T0278827

Elite • 253

Anglo-Saxon Kings and Warlords

AD 400–1070

**RAFFAELE D'AMATO &
STEPHEN POLLINGTON**

ILLUSTRATED BY RAFFAELE RUGGERI

Series editors Martin Windrow & Nick Reynolds

OSPREY PUBLISHING
Bloomsbury Publishing plc
Kemp House, Chawley Park, Cumnor Hill, Oxford OX2 9PH, UK
29 Earlsfort Terrace, Dublin 2, Ireland
1385 Broadway, Fifth Floor, New York, NY 10018, USA
E-mail: info@ospreypublishing.com
www.ospreypublishing.com

OSPREY is a trademark of Osprey Publishing Ltd
First published in Great Britain in 2023

© Osprey Publishing Ltd 2023

A catalogue record for this book is available from the British Library

ISBN: PB 9781472855350; eBook: 9781472855343; ePDF: 9781472855367
XML: 9781472855336

23 24 25 26 27 10 9 8 7 6 5 4 3 2 1

Editor: Martin Windrow
Index by Fionbar Lyons
Typeset by PDQ Digital Media Solutions, Bungay, UK
Printed and bound in India by Replika Press Private Ltd.

MIX
Paper from
responsible sources
FSC® C016779
www.fsc.org

Osprey Publishing supports the Woodland Trust, the UK's leading woodland
conservation charity.

To find out more about our authors and books, visit
www.ospreypublishing.com. Here you will find extracts, author interviews,
details of forthcoming events, and the option to sign up for our newsletter.

Dedication
To the English people – a nation of sailors, warriors and adventurers

Acknowledgements
Preparing this book has required the intensive collaboration of friends,
colleagues, museums and other institutions in collecting the necessary
information and iconography. We express our sincere gratitude, to old
friends and new, for generously putting their resources at our disposal:
In Britain, to Brett Hammond, Chris Wren, and the library of Timeline
Auctions for essential access to British archaeological publications; and to
Matt Bunker, for valuable advice and much generous photographic help.
Paul Mortimer, one of the pioneers of Anglo-Saxon re-enactment and
experimental archaeology, also helped us with unpublished photographic
material.
Many British museums and other institutions contributed generously to
the illustrations, as will be seen in the credits. In alphabetical order they are:
All Saints' Parish in Bakewell, All Saints' Church in Brailsford, the
Archaeology Data Service (ADS), the British Library, the British Museum, the
Corpus of Anglo-Saxon Sculptures, the Church of St Mary & St Barlock in
Norbury, Derby Archaeological Museum, Dorset County Museum in
Dorchester, Ipswich City Museum, Kendal Museum, the Lewes Museum at
Alfriston, the Portable Antiquity Scheme (PAS), Preston Park Museum in
Stockton-on-Tees, Sheffield City Museum, Timeline Auctions, Tullie House
Museum & Art Gallery Trust, Winchester Library and Winchester City
Museum, and the Yorkshire Museum. We also record our gratitude to
Jeroen Punt, curator of the Netherlands National Military Museum at Delft,
and to the Metropolitan Museum, New York.
For the graphic and computer enhancement of the published images, we
are indebted in respect of the hard work of Dr Marco Saliola, and for
drawings, as so often, to Dr Andrea Salimbeti. The reconstruction colour
plates for this book were particularly challenging, and we especially
acknowledge the talent, skill and great patience of the artist
Raffaele Ruggeri.
Raffaele D'Amato
Stephen Pollington

Title page photo
Detail from the 8th-century Franks Casket, a Northumbrian whalebone
chest which illustrates contemporary Anglo-Saxon warriors. See page 40.
(British Museum; photo Raffaele D'Amato, courtesy the Museum)

Artist's note
Readers may care to note that the original paintings from which the colour
plates in this book were prepared are available for private sale. All
reproduction copyright whatsoever is retained by the publishers. All
enquiries should be addressed to:
raffaele.ruggeri@alice.it
The publishers regret that they can enter into no correspondence upon this
matter.

CONTENTS

ANGLO-SAXON KINGS AND WARLORDS, AD 400–1070

INTRODUCTION

Among the influx of peoples who invaded sub-Roman and post-Roman Britannia in the 5th–7th centuries AD, the Angles *(Engle)*, Jutes *(Eote)*, Mercians, Saxons *(Seaxe)*, Franks, Danes and *Svear-Sweonas* (Swedish) were all represented. United by common or related Germanic languages, they later came to describe themselves collectively as 'Anglo-Saxons', speaking the language we call Old English.

Perhaps the first Germanic-speaking settlers had been retired members of the Roman-employed military, who formed *coloniae* around Roman military strongholds and depended for their status on the continued prestige of the Roman Empire. There is evidence for depopulation across much of lowland Britain in the later 3rd century, and for the subsequent settlement in the Midlands of *foederati* – men who undertook a contract or treaty *(foedus)* to work for the Roman authorities, bringing in their families and contributing an agricultural workforce to replenish the tax-base of the Late Roman economy in the 4th century. Certainly, the European upheavals and constant warfare of that century also provided

The 'Warham rider' from Norfolk, 4th–6th century. This rather stylized copper-alloy figurine may depict an early Anglian leader on horseback. It differs from examples of similar subjects known from the Roman period, and an early Anglo-Saxon date is therefore preferred. The closest parallel to this find is the more detailed early Anglo-Saxon 'gaming piece' figurine from Bradwell, Norfolk (NMS-40A7A7), which shows a horse with similar proportions (see page 44). The Warham find measures 28mm/1.1ins long, 31mm/1.2ins high and 7.5mm/0.29ins thick, and weighs 14.22g/0.5 ounces. (PAS record NMS-32FEA3, licence CC BY-SA 4.0)

a ready supply of prisoners-of-war, whose labour could be harnessed to maintain the output of food and materials from the villa estates of Britain and northern Gaul at a time when the workforce was diminished by successive plagues and uprisings.

The Romans routinely enlisted defeated enemies to fight for them, and so, during a period when mobile field units were being withdrawn by commanders in Britain attempting to usurp Imperial power (Magnus Maximus in the late 4th century, and Constantine III in the early 5th), they also used such men to stiffen Britain's static border garrisons *(limitanei)* of hereditary local recruits, who had to resist Pictish and Irish attacks. But it was only with the removal of the impediment of Roman nominal authority and tax-gathering after about 410 that hereditary elites can be said to have appeared among these immigrants.

We may query whether such early named figures as Hengest and Sigeferth truly existed, or were simply drawn from folklore, but the point is that successive generations of Angles, Jutes and others believed that these had been real historical leaders. Such elites were clearly energetic and adaptable, bringing not only military vigour but also new ideas about social and religious organization to a Roman-dependant state which had come to the brink of collapse.

A common idea about the Anglo-Saxon period was that the military was not as glamorous or effective as those of their enemies: Romanised Celtic Britons, and later Vikings and Normans. This misapprehension stems from the Victorian obsessions with the Classical world, and romantic ideas of 'noble savages' drawn from the emerging science of anthropology. Generally, finds of Anglo-Saxon material could not be identified with certainty in the archaeological record, with the result that any relatively crude or badly degraded material was considered 'British', while any finely-made or beautiful finds were ascribed to the Romans.

Decades of scholarly study made only small inroads into this false impression – indeed, it has not been entirely overturned to this day. However, more recent archaeological discoveries have provided a wealth of counter-evidence. The 'Taplow mound' in Buckinghamshire, with its fine metalwork and glassware, was recognized as Anglo-Saxon upon its discovery in the 1880s, but it remained for decades the only high-status burial assemblage attributed to them. Since the excavation of the famous ship burial at Sutton Hoo in Suffolk in 1939, scholars have of course had to accept a completely different reality.

Details of a sword from grave 22 in the Blacknall Field cemetery, Pewsey, Wiltshire, dated to the second half of the 5th century. The site yielded a number of high-status warrior burials, and frequent evidence of blade wounds. Here laid on a pinkish-brown background with numbered labels, this sword was associated with a copper-alloy 'cocked-hat' pommel, a scabbard mouth-piece decorated in 'quoit brooch' style, and U-section scabbard edging embossed on one side and decorated with gold leaf and silver strips, while the blade retained substantial traces of the original wooden scabbard. A leather strap passed around the scabbard through the bindings, and attached it to the wearer's belt. The sword was found together with an iron shield boss and related fastening rivets and iron grip, a copper-alloy fastener fitting, a socketed iron spearhead, an iron buckle with a silver and gilt copper-alloy plate, and an iron knife and chape. (Photos courtesy Matt Bunker)

SELECT CHRONOLOGY (AD)

c.449 Invited into Britain as military allies, the Jutish leaders Hengest and Horsa establish the first Anglo-Saxon settlement in the south-east – the event called by Bede the *Adventus Saxonum* (HE, I, 15). Violent and usually successful wars of expansion soon follow.

c.516 Battle of Badon Hill: post-Roman Celtic elite temporarily defeat the Saxon advance into western Britain.

597 Pope Gregory I sends a Christian mission to the Anglian King Æthelbert of Kent, then the overlord of all the Anglo-Saxon kingdoms south of the river Humber.

c.616 King Æthelfrith of Bernicia (Northumbria) defeats the Britons ('Welsh') of Powys and Gwynned at Chester, but is himself defeated and killed in Nottinghamshire by King Rædwald of East Anglia.

c.625 Burial of King Rædwald at Sutton Hoo, Suffolk.

655 After long wars against the rival Saxon dynasty of Northumbria, the last great pagan Anglo-Saxon king, Penda of Mercia (the modern Midlands) is killed at the battle of Winwæd.

664 The Synod of Whitby recognizes the sole authority of Rome in matters of Christian practice.

731 Bede completes his *Historia Ecclesiastica Gentis Anglorum*.

757–796 Reign of Offa of Mercia, 'king and glory of Britain'.

793 First recorded major Scandinavian raid, on the island of Lindisfarne, Northumbria.

796 Battle of Rhuddlan; Offa defeats the Welsh, and overcomes all Britain south of the Humber.

835 Norse raid on Kent begins almost annual Viking attacks on British coasts and extending inland.

864/865 The Danish 'great army' first remains in Britain over the winter – thus raiders become settlers.

871 King Ælfred of Wessex (Alfred the Great, r. 871–899) defeats the Danes at the battle of Ashdown.

Sculpture from a cross-shaft from Norbury near Ashbourne, Derbyshire, depicting an elite warrior, *c.*AD 900. While possibly representing the Norse god Heimdal, blowing his horn to mark the beginning of Ragnarök, it does not have Scandinavian design features, and the crested helmet and pleated skirt show affinity with Anglo-Saxon and Carolingian models. The carving on this 'Norbury Stone' seems to represent a padded armour perhaps reinforced with metallic discs or embellished with round ornaments. (*in situ*, Church of St Mary & St Barlock, Norbury; photo Raffaele D'Amato, courtesy of the parish)

From the first, the leaders of Germanic war-bands and the petty kingdoms that evolved from them were frequently engaged personally in physical combat, as well as in deploying their forces and organizing the structure of their territories. They and their elite followers distinguished themselves through displays of wealth and military splendour symbolic of their strength, prowess and fitness to lead. The Anglo-Saxon elite was magnificently fitted out with a mixture of equipment influenced by the contemporary cultures of the Late Romans, Scandinavians of the Vendel and later Viking periods, continental Merovingians, Carolingians and

879	Alfred decisively defeats the Danes at Edington. Danish leader Guthrum accepts Christianity with Alfred as his sponsor, and the Viking army leaves Wessex.
886 *et seq:*	Alfred, now 'King of the Anglo-Saxons', establishes limits of agreed Danish administration in eastern and northern England (for which the term the 'Danelaw' dates only from the 11th century). Alfred builds a network of *burh* fortified towns/strongholds across southern Britain. The marriage of his daughter Æthelflæd cements the alliance of Wessex with Mercia.
*c.*911 *et seq:*	Alfred's son Edward the Elder, and the widowed Æthelflæd ('The Lady of the Mercians'), extend the burgh network into Essex, East Anglia and the Midlands.
937	Alfred's grandson Athelstan, first king of all England, decisively defeats an Irish–Norse–Scottish alliance at the battle of Brunanburh. Aggressive Viking activity in England ceases for more than half a century.
991	Battle at Maldon, Essex: defeat by Vikings of Anglo-Saxons under the *ealdorman* Byrhtnoth, during reign of King Æthelred 'the Unready' ('the Ill-Advised').
1002	Provoked by Viking raids, despite payment of 'Danegeld' to buy off attacks, Æthelred orders a massacre of Danish inhabitants in his territory. King Sweyn Forkbeard of Denmark begins a decade of vengeful attacks.
1016–1035	Sweyn's son Cnut (Canute) the Great rules his North Sea empire from England, as king of all England, Denmark, Norway and part of Sweden.
1042 *et seq:*	After the deaths of Cnut's sons, Æthelred's son Edward the Confessor soon succeeds to the throne.
1066	After Edward's death without an heir, both King Harald Hardrada of Norway (unsuccessfully) and Duke William of Normandy contest the succession to the English throne of Harold Godwineson, Earl of Wessex. The latter's defeat and death at the hands of William's army at Hastings brings an end to English independence.

Ottonians, as well as their own customary forms of display in costume, textiles, weaponry, horse-harness, and much else besides. Anglo-Saxon rulers, warlords and churchmen interacted with their contemporary equivalents across continental Europe and Scandinavia by diplomacy, trade, intermarriage and military intervention. Their culture was neither static nor constrained by traditions, but rather was willing to engage with new ideas, new processes and new materials. When the 8th-century King Offa of Mercia corresponded with the Frankish king and future Holy Roman Emperor Charlemagne, he did so as a fellow Christian monarch of an energetic and powerful early mediaeval state.

The purpose of this book is to show how the Anglo-Saxon elite presented itself on the battlefield and for ceremonial occasions. Beside the archaeology, as always, we have drawn upon the literary evidence (the so-called *Anglo-Saxon Chronicle*, Christian writings, later transcriptions of early heroic poetry, and legal documents), and the iconography, though the latter is scarce before the 11th century. Luckily for us, until at least the mid-7th century the Anglo-Saxons buried their dead with their personal possessions and weapons.

THE ANGLO-SAXON ELITE

Historical background

Development of Anglo-Saxon rulership and the establishment of kingdoms took place over a long period of time, from the first creation of settlements on the eastern and southern coasts of Britain in the 450s AD, through the growth of petty and then regional kingdoms, until the formation of a single English realm in the early 10th century.

According to the British cleric Gildas, the *Saxones* had their origins as pagan Germanic warriors who had entered Britain after the Roman field army left early in the 5th century, and settled in the south-east under a treaty with the local Romano-British authorities. There is little reason to doubt this interpretation, given that the Late Romans had imported mercenaries from at least the mid-4th century onwards. In a single passage Gildas gives his understanding of the nature of this *foedus* (treaty), correctly using several Late Roman terms associated with the temporary settlement of allies on Roman territory in return for military service.

The origins of kingship among the peoples who would eventually style themselves 'Anglo-Saxons' lie deep in the prehistory of their societies. Their immediate geographical origins may be found in the area of the North Sea rim in the last centuries BC, although any records of this period are difficult to interpret: archaeological complexes can seldom be matched up to what the scant written sources have to tell us. Tribal names such as 'Cimbri' and 'Teutones' appear occasionally, but it is only with the work of a Roman historian and politician – Publius Cornelius Tacitus, writing in the late 1st

A **ADVENTUS SAXONUM, c. AD 449**

(1) Hengest the exile

The legendary Jutish leader is imagined as wearing a helmet of *spangenhelm* construction in gilded iron and copper-alloy, here copied from the 5th-century Gultlingen specimen now in the Stuttgart State Museum. The iron ring-mail armour (*byrne* or *byrnie*) is decorated with edging bands of copper-alloy rings. It is worn over clothing copied from finds in Danish bogs; a long tunic (*cyrtel*) is covered by a short-sleeved *overcyrtel*, with trousers from the Thorsberg find, and over all he wears a fringed, chequered cloak. The massive belt buckle (from Mucking, Essex) is decorated in the 'quoit-brooch' fashion which combined Romano-Celtic and Germanic styles. The sword he carries is copied from the incomplete Abingdon specimen, with missing elements taken from the Selmeston find.

(2) Sigeferth, lord of the Secgan

Another warrior exile, Sigeferth was supposedly a friend of Hengest who shared in his adventures in Frisia, and defended him when the hall they shared was attacked (a story told in *Beowulf* and in *The Fight at Finnsburg*). He wears the 'pillbox' Pannonian cap which was apparently adopted from the Late Roman military. His sleeveless fur jerkin (*pād*) is gathered at the waist by a broad leather belt with a buckle derived from Roman military types, the strap end having a copper-alloy knop. The belt supports a pouch with a firesteel on the lower edge of the flap, and a light axe. His pale linen tunic is decorated with bands of applied textile decoration, and he

wears a *beag* (arm-ring) on each wrist. His tight-fitting woollen trousers are bound round the lower legs with puttee-like linen strips, and a short knife is slipped into the bindings at his right knee. The spear is of the *angon* type, with a long iron shank and a barbed head. The convex shield displays a pointed iron boss and leather-bound rim, with studs on the face where carrying/slinging straps are secured inside. Its blazon is based on the iconography of gold bracteate medallions of the period.

(3) Vortigern, post-Roman British *Dux*

This British leader, who supposedly invited the Jutish warlords Hengest and Horsa into south-east England, wears Late Roman military-style clothing as a mark of his status, copied from the possibly 5th-century *Vergilius Romanus* codex miniatures. His white woollen tunic features applied textile bands and panels *(clavi)* with rich embroidery. His heavy cloak is dyed a rich blueish-purple and fastened at his right shoulder; above its edge note a gold *torque* neck-ring. His sword belts and scabbard are of dyed leather and the hilt of his *spatha*-type sword is ivory, both with gilded copper-alloy fittings; the pommel is of the 'cocked hat' shape (so called for a supposed resemblance to the shape of Napoleon's bicorne). The woollen saddlecloth is dyed Imperial purple and embroidered with gold thread in Roman military style. The helmet he holds is of classic Late Roman ridge-helm typology, with coloured glass or gemstone ornaments; it is reconstructed from the Richborough fragment and based on the Budapest example, and has a purple-dyed horsehair crest.

1

2

3

The famous 'Spong Hill man', a figurine measuring 14cm/5½ins high decorating the lid of a cremation urn found in the Anglian cemetery at Spong Hill, Norfolk. It is currently the only known representation of an Anglo-Saxon warrior of the 5th century, dressed in elements of Late Roman military costume such as the 'pillbox' cap known as the *pileus pannonicus*. (ex Pollington, Kerr & Hammond; image, Lindsay Kerr, 2010)

century AD – that some light is shed on the disposition and distinguishing features of tribes in northern Europe.

It is Tacitus's work *De origine et situ Germanorum* ('On the Origin and Placement of the Germans') that first mentions the Anglian tribe *(Anglii)*, forming part of a cultic league worshipping a goddess whose image was carried around their region in an ox-wagon. Tacitus's text is not a dispassionate ethnographic work, but rather a presentation of curiosities, facts and opinions; he describes the *Germanii* as typical savage peoples, but therefore uncorrupted by luxury, being loyal, fierce and warlike.

Tacitus has little to say about the details of rulership among these tribes, although we do learn that 'kings' were chosen for their nobility of birth while 'warlords' were appointed for their abilities: *reges ex nobilitate, duces ex virtutes (Germania, Ch.7)*. This division of authority may have been traditional in the 1st century, but it was not to last. During the immense economic, social and political upheavals of the 3rd–5th centuries which saw the decline of Roman power in north-west Europe, new leaders came to the fore. Noble birth no longer guaranteed leadership, whereas the ability to plan, to inspire followers, and to seize opportunities to make and abandon alliances became critical.

The military immigration of the early 5th century soon led to rebellions against local post-Roman rulers, and competitive struggles for ever-expanding territories between Germanic war-bands that quickly evolved into minor kingdoms. The ability to seize and hold territory was vital to success. Even the small early kingdoms were largely new creations without direct descent from previous institutions (other than in Kent); and the larger kingdoms that would emerge subsequently (Wessex, Mercia and Northumbria) were built on the remains of earlier, smaller units (e.g. Bernicia, Rheged, Deira, Elmet, etc). While the identities they created in Britain might echo old names (East, South and West Saxons relating to continental groups of the same names), there is no evidence from the grave-goods of any exclusivity along ethnic lines: for instance, Wessex contained Saxon settlers, but also Franks and Jutes. Only the East Angles retained their nominal link with the folk of *Angeln*, while similar relationships were no longer actively maintained in Northumbria and Mercia. Bede's neat division of the Germanic settlers into Angles, Saxons and Jutes corresponds to the larger picture in the archaeology – Anglian types of grave-goods do appear where he stated that Angles settled – but in almost every cemetery there are intrusive elements from other cultures, and also some which seem blended.

Kings embodied their peoples, representing them in dealing with the supernatural and with other kings. There was a numinous quality to kingship,

Gold 5th-century bracteate medallion from Undley, Suffolk. This complex object, bearing what may be the earliest attested words in English, represents a warrior wearing a pseudo-Attic helmet recalling Roman iconography. Note too the image of the she-wolf suckling Romulus and Remus; the wolf was also a totemic beast of the Germanic peoples. (ex Pollington, Kerr & Hammond; image, Lindsay Kerr, 2010)

and the king himself could adopt a god-like role in certain circumstances: donning the war-helm would probably be a good example. It was no accident that the Christian missionary effort was directed at kings and royal courts: the god of the king was *de facto* the god of the people, because the king had to intercede with the deity on their behalf.

Elite relationships

In Britain and elsewhere in post-Roman Europe, a new breed of rulers emerged whose authority was not founded on any institution but rather on the personal loyalty of powerful men and women. Predominant among these was the figure of the 'ætheling' (*æðeling*), a prince or lord from a noble family that had a claim to leadership. The social structure which these societies developed was based on personal duties and obligations, on rewards and incentives, on public displays of honour and of shame. The central social institution for these new warlords and their followers was the 'meadhall', the centre of social and public life for the lord (*frea*) and his people. The meadhall was an imposing physical structure of sturdy rectangular construction with benches along the long walls, usually a central long-fire, an imposing doorway, and at the far end a raised dais from which the leader could oversee his people and be seen by them.

On the benches were seated his young followers, who traditionally were drawn from different communities, and hoped to win by their service praise and rewards – visible symbols of success such as swords and other weapons, gold, jewels, goblets, drinking horns, horses and harness. The young men slept in the hall, but followed the lord on his progress around his territory,

Cast silver-gilt mount, perhaps part of a buckle, representing a warrior's face with helmet; AD 450–500, probably Scandinavian-made. This fitting, measuring 4.8cm x 2.2cm (1.9ins x 0.86ins). shows several anthropomorphic images, one of which is cast in the round. It has a thick brow with a large protruding nose, and a ridge running up to the hairline or headdress, which might indicate a half-face mask similar to an image on a fitting from Aldborough, Yorkshire. (PAS record NLM-219C93, licence CC BY-SA 4.0)

and especially onto the battlefield, where they hoped to win not just physical rewards but also individual renown and advancement. Apart from those locals with close personal ties to the lord, their service might be for a fixed term – one summer, for example, or the duration of a military campaign – after which they might set out in search of another leader. If the rewards had been good enough already, they might perhaps return to their homes and marry, take up a parcel of land, and achieve a more settled life. Those who chose to stay with the lord would join the troop of reliable and experienced warriors who provided leadership in battle and maintained order in the ranks.

A leader's authority was based ultimately on two factors: the possibility of reward and the prospect of punishment. Loyal followers could expect to earn generous gifts and public recognition for their service – as long as the man they followed was lucky, rich, and inclined to distribute his disposable wealth. A lord who did not share out the benefits of his followers' successes would earn a reputation for meanness – a 'wolfish heart', as one poet put it – and would not be able to attract hardy and ambitious youngsters to follow him. If a leader fell from power, he might no longer have the means to reward his companions, and this would be the test of whether the brave words of loyalty spoken in the hall were meant seriously or were empty boasts. Disloyalty could be punished by banishment and exile, and the life of an exile was never easy. Since he had proved himself either unworthy or incapable of carrying out his promises, his record would hardly recommend him to another prospective leader.

The loyal band of followers was known in Old English as the *werod* ('protective force') or the *gedriht* ('band of men sworn to share hardship together'), under the command of a warlord (OE *dryhten* or *drihten*). Similar groups among Late Rome's barbarian allies had already emerged and imposed themselves on agricultural populations across Europe – Goths in Rumania and Ukraine, Marcomanni along the Danube, Batavi in the Netherlands – all of them societies with a militarized elite.

In Britain these traditional structures based upon personal loyalties between rulers and followers were subject to great strain in the long 9th-century wars against the Danish Vikings. However, in the latter part of that century Alfred of Wessex (r. 871–899), the last remaining independent Saxon kingdom, undertook a wholesale re-organization of the military and wider duties of the elite. In his reforms the status of thane (OE *þegn*, pl. *þegnas* – a landowner with military obligations, roughly similar to those of a later feudal knight) was restricted to men who not only had proven military accomplishments, but who could read; literacy was to be one key to Alfred's successes. Another was the establishment of a growing network of fortified towns (*burhs*/burghs) governed by his trusted subordinates.

Structure

The word thane meant 'one who serves', and might describe either an aristocratic individual retainer of a king or senior nobleman or, as a class term, the majority of the aristocracy below the ranks of *ealdormen* and high-reeves (see below). They served their royal lords in peacetime as well as war, and appear in the sources as tax administrators, enforcers of the king's laws and dispensers of justice through the courts, witnesses to royal charters, recipients of land grants, and donors of land in their turn.

While such careers might begin as simple bodyguards in the *werod* (8th-century sources refer to them as *gesíþas*, 'companions' of the king), the subsequent development of medieval-style kingship might see them rise to become high-ranking *ealdormen* (sing. *ealdorman*) or 'regional governors' administering a whole territory (OE *scīr*, 'shire'). As the 9th-century kingdom of Wessex expanded to include most of southern Britain, new shires based around economic hubs or military strongholds were established (e.g. Oxfordshire based on Oxford, Hertfordshire on Hertford, and so on).

Anglo-Saxon military mounts, 6th century. (Top left) Copper-alloy shield boss apex disc from Cambridgeshire. (Centre) Shield mount, gold and silver surface finish, from grave 600, Mucking, Essex. (Bottom) Chip-carved shield mount, gilt copper-alloy, from Melton Mowbray, Leicestershire. (ex Pollington, Kerr & Hammond, 2010)

The *ealdorman* was the highest grade of official. The title is not mentioned in the Kentish laws, and perhaps such a small kingdom did not require this level of authority in the early days. The *ealdorman* appears to be well established in Wessex by the time of Ine (r. 689–726), and is probably the rank for which Stephen of Ripon (Eddius Stephanus) uses the Latin terms *subregulus* and *princeps*. However, it is never easy to equate the terms in Latin sources with those in Old English. For instance, Brihtfrith, a *princeps* in Stephen's work, is called a *prefectus* by Bede, whose use of *princeps* may be confined to men of royal blood. Bede also seems to use *dux* for *ealdorman* when used in its sense of military leader. *Prefectus* is generally used for *gerefa* or 'reeve', but the retention of the title 'high-reeve' in the North for the rulers of Bamburgh (one of whom is given the title 'king' in a Celtic source) may suggest that in early times *gerefa* had a wider application and was not used only of officials inferior to the *ealdorman*.

In the attestations to early West Saxon charters, *prefectus* seems to be used for *ealdorman*. From the second half of the 9th century, *ealdorman* is also rendered as the Latin *comes*, but in earlier writers such as Bede this word probably translates to the Old English *gesiþ*. Occasionally one reads the term *patricius*, perhaps of an *ealdorman* holding a particularly influential position (in sub-Roman Gaul it was the title of a regional Imperial viceroy). In the 11th century the native word *ealdorman* was ousted under Scandinavian influence by *jarl*, 'earl'.

Thanes may be characterized as a group of 'ministers' (officers) and attendants upon the king whose duties extended from the palace to the battlefield. Thus we find the same man described as a *cyngeshuskarl* ('king's housecarl') in one charter, and as a *'minister regis'* ('officer of the king') in another. Even from early times there is evidence of the king and greater nobles employing *milites stipendiis* or mercenary warriors brought in to strengthen an army, serving for an agreed and limited period. When witnessing land-grants, the Latin term *miles* ('soldier') was sometimes used for men of thanely status, but also *minister,* implying that the rank of thane was never purely military in nature.

By the later Anglo-Saxon period, it appears that the link between land-holding and the rank of thane had become weakened. The sons and grandsons of *ceorls* ('yeomen') who had become thanes were entitled to retain the rank; it had become hereditary, and thus detached from land-holding and merit acquired through personal service. By the time of the *Domesday* census in 1086 there were many 'thanes' who had estates far smaller than the statutory (in Wessex) five hides. (The 'hide' was a variable measurement of the taxable value of the land necessary to support one family.)

Successful leadership was exercised through practical example, so a leader (*folctoga*) of a military force raised in a single district *(folc)* was expected to have a set of skills which were not available to everyone. In the pre-Christian period lordship was very much bound up with the cult of the god Woden, who appears as the actual founder of many royal families in the king-lists. Woden means 'the lord of inspiration', and the god passed on secret

B KING ÆTHELBERT OF KENT, c.AD 600

(1) King Æthelbert

The king wears a helmet based on the example from Benty Grange, Derbyshire, which bears a crest in the shape of a boar, but also has a Christian cross added to the nasal in silver studs; note that he also displays a pectoral cross on a gold chain around his neck. He has a trimmed moustache and beard and shoulder-length hair, in the style shown on the Sutton Hoo sceptre. His knee-length linen tunic has decorated edging bands and is gathered at the waist with a woven fabric belt with a gold clasp. He wears a bleached white (Latin, *alba*) cloak also with braid edging, fastened at the right shoulder; the brooch might resemble the example from Wijnaldum, Netherlands, which was then Frankish territory. His sword, copied from the Cumberland specimen, is slung at his left hip from a baldric with a small buckle, and a small knife hangs across the front of his waist belt. His equipment is decorated with Germanic Style I motifs (Salin's classification). His horse harness, in crimson leather with gilded copper-alloy fittings, is copied from the Faversham finds, integrated with different equestrian elements recovered in England.

(2) Kentish *gesið* warlord

This warlord accompanying his king is a man of rank and wealth, and we copy his equipment largely from the contemporary princely burial at Prittlewell, Essex. We give him a helmet based on the Shorwell specimen but with restored cheek-guards. His mailcoat is worn over a short woollen tunic with braid decoration at the collar, sleeve-ends and hem, over a similarly-decorated long-sleeved tunic. In his right hand he holds a sword with the braided belt wrapped around the scabbard, and in his left his leather-covered wooden shield. He has a throwing-axe (*francisca*) tucked into his belt.

(3) Merovingian Frankish comes

Leading families on both sides of the Channel maintained close ties, and we show this Frankish warlord as if visiting the Kentish court. We copy his appearance from the Bradwell horseman figurine, but have given him a glass 'claw beaker', which he offers to the king as a stirrup-cup. His belt is fastened with a large iron buckle with silver ornament, copied from Frankish grave finds. His sword and knife are worn at his left hip. He holds an angon spear with carved decoration on the shaft, from the Prittlewell princely grave. His shield is copied from a find at Bidford-on-Avon (grave 182), with applications in silver and gilded copper alloy.

The 10th-century Skerne sword is an unusually fine example of a pattern-welded blade with a decorated hilt, the pommel and guard being inlaid with silver and copper wires in geometric designs. It was found during excavations of a waterlogged site near Driffield, East Yorkshire in 1982 by the Humberside Archaeology Unit; it had been dropped, complete with its scabbard, into the river Hull. (Hull Museum collections; photo courtesy of Matt Bunker)

knowledge to his chosen worshippers, partly through intoxicants. Among the secrets which the kingly class had to learn were strategies of battle; these were practised and rehearsed through board games where the objective is to capture the opponent's 'king', and in hunting wild animals.

Literacy, then a rare attribute, was another powerful tool available to those who worshipped Woden in heathen times. The advent of Christianity in the 7th century brought exposure to Latin literacy, although it did not spread widely among the laity. In the later 9th century, as mentioned, the ability to read (in English rather than Latin) was one of the requirements for senior service under Alfred. Obviously, it would have been a powerful aid to his governance to be able to send clear and detailed instructions to subordinates. The skills of reading and writing are not the same, however, and composition (writing) was restricted to a small number of clerics and officials whose task it was to coordinate the management of the kingdom. These *ministri* were highly accomplished and often very cultured, with a wide knowledge of Latin and other authors from antiquity to more recent times.

Warrior qualities and expectations

The 10th-century poem *The Wanderer*, describing the life of an exiled warrior in search of a new lord to serve, specifies the qualities which were expected of a prudent man: 'A wise man must be patient, must not be too hot-headed nor too hasty in speech, neither too bashful in battle nor too blindly reckless, neither too craven nor too carefree, nor too keen for wealth, nor ever too fond of boasting before he fully understands.' The recommendation of such qualities of moderation indicates that headlong aggression was as undesirable as laziness or timidity in a warrior, who had to be a 'team player' if he and his group were to survive.

Warfare was usually conducted in order to gain access to scarce resources: territory, and the subsequent output of its subject population; livestock, and slaves. A less quantifiable but arguably more important resource was prestige or honour (OE *weorþ*). Among highly competitive groups the victorious warrior stood to gain prestige from his attacks against the enemy – witnessed by his fellow warriors and his superiors – while also acquiring economic benefit in the form of booty, and rewards from a grateful leader. The receiving of valuable weapons was one of the most desired warrior rewards; by performing brave deeds with his existing weapons, he showed himself ready and able to perform greater deeds with better armament. Likewise, a leader who appeared on the battlefield with lavish equipment displayed himself as ready for combat and capable of taking a leading part in it. His appearance was therefore part of his social identity: richly-furnished weapons and war-gear formed part of the social display which marked out leaders, noblemen and warriors from other ranks of society.

Fosterage, and the meadhall

Central to military life were two important customs: the system of fosterage, and gatherings in the meadhall.

Under the former, boys of suitable temperament whose families had the means to support them were placed in the household of a social superior. There they performed menial duties, such as serving at table, cleaning weapons, repairing equipment, grooming horses, etc; these taught them how to behave courteously, the basics of how to care for gear and animals, and how to handle weapons with respect. Games of wrestling and running built strength. Hunting and horse-racing improved co-ordination and taught the youngster tactics – how to chase a stag or boar, to wear it out and to corner it effectively. Beyond this, the boys who were selected for future leadership roles would learn about strategy, diplomacy, coercion and other skills that would be needed when the boy became an experienced fighter (known collectively in OE as *duguð*), capable of leading a group of warriors of his own.

The meadhall was the social centre of its community – the place where discussions took place among leaders and their men and between guests and host; where rewards were handed out and gifts exchanged; where promises were made, and reputations enhanced by the praise-songs of poets (*scopas*). Before the advent of Christianity it was also the religious centre where rituals in honour of the gods were enacted. It was the mustering point for the military before campaigns began; the storehouse of food and wealth; and the administrative centre for the district – the place where important decisions were taken, where the law was enforced and judgements given. For the elite, it was the stage on which they demonstrated their renown and authority. The elaborate decorated drinking horns found in the Sutton Hoo and Prittlewell graves, among others, were also social symbols used in the meadhall, and were probably carried while on horseback on long military campaigns.

By the end of the Anglo-Saxon period the meadhall had begun to lose its institutional importance: its religious role was taken over by the church, its defensive role by the *burh* stronghold, and its economic role by the mint. But in the Anglo-Saxon imagination it remained the centre where all that was good in life could be found.

Ritual single combat

Among warriors it was customary to avoid unnecessary bloodshed by settling disputes by means of single combat between champions.

The Wareham sword, late 10th century, found in the river Frome in 1927; the hilt and roughly half the blade survives, with signs of intricate decoration in copper alloy and silver on the guard and pommel. Its main interest lies in the remains of an inscription on the horn grip: translated, it reads 'Æthel-[…] owns me'. Names beginning 'Æthel-'('noble') were frequent among members of the royal family and nobility of Wessex; this sword is the only one known which is named to an individual warlord. (Dorset County Museum, Dorchester; photo courtesy of Matt Bunker)

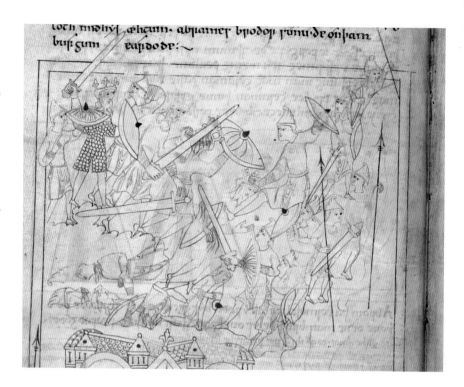

'Abraham slaughtering the Kings of Elam', from a mid-or late-11th-century manuscript miniature. The only warrior protected by a ringmail hauberk seems to be Abraham (top left), depicted as an 11th-century Anglo-Saxon ruler; at his right side is the shield-bearer defending him. The swords represented here seem to echo Types S and X of Petersen's classification (1919), perhaps with gilded pommels and guards. (British Library, MS Cotton Claudius IV, folio 24v; photo courtesy of the Library)

This ritualized warfare was governed by strict rules, the breaking of which meant loss of honour. Some groups used this form of fighting to test their war-luck before entering into battle, by capturing one of the enemy and forcing him to fight one of their own men; Tacitus says (*Germania*, Ch.10) that the outcome of the duel could be used to settle the differences between whole nations, implicitly therefore without further loss of life. Yet an army which found that its luck was out – that the gods were favouring its opponents – would still have to choose whether to enter into battle or buy peace by paying tribute.

The duel was simply a single combat fought between two opponents, each armed with sword and shield. In Norse tradition this was known as *hólmganga*, 'going to an island', since the normally selected site was away from interference or assistance by other parties. From the literature it seems that fair play and an exchange of strokes, turn and turn about, was the norm. A man could refuse to fight if challenged, but risked public ridicule and loss of credibility if he did so.

ARMIES

Werod and *húskarlar*

The *werod* was originally the king's small bodyguard of sworn retainers whose duty it was to follow him in peace and war, and to enforce his will. In the early period, following a tradition originating in the Iron Age, the *werod* arose from the personal relationship between king and retainer. With enlargement of the surviving major kingdoms (reduced from seven to three) during the Danish wars, the original modest-sized retinue of royal guards assumed wider responsibility for defence and government.

The later institution of the *húskarlar* was introduced by the 11th-century Danish king Cnut (Canute) as a personal following without ties to the English state. The *húskarlar* (Old Norse, 'household-men') were armed with fine weapons and armour including swords and mailcoats. We are told that Cnut required his housecarls to possess 'splendid armour', and a double-edged sword with a gold-inlaid hilt, as a condition of acceptance into his military entourage. The housecarl is also associated with the two-handed battleaxe, which characterized such warriors. Despite being paid in coin – they were 'stipendiary troops' – their obligation to serve in arms arose from the lordship-bond of duty rather than any cash inducement.

The size of the armies available to Anglo-Saxon kings has often been understated, partly due to a passage in the laws of King Ine of Wessex (r. 689–726) telling us that a group of up to seven men were called *ðeofas*, 'thieves'; from seven to 35, a *hloþ* 'band'; and above that number a *here*, 'army'. The specific circumstances of Ine's reign, when he perceived a threat from the presence of large armed groups outside his control, encouraged him to limit the size of the military forces available to his individual *ealdormen*. More generally, however, military forces were as large as the state could afford – few kings were so confident in the abilities of their men that they would willingly take the field with any smaller force.

The Staffordshire Hoard

We have the evidence of the 7th-century Staffordshire Hoard to weigh against Ine's legal limitations. This hoard consists of as many as 3,500 metal items, all in gold or silver and many finely decorated with garnet-filled *cloisons* (flat cells); the total weight after excavation is estimated to be about 5kg/11lbs of gold and 1.3kg/2.8lbs of silver. Almost all the items are fragments of military equipment. A processional cross and some other puzzling fittings

Fragmentary plaque from the Staffordshire Hoard, item 595, representing a warrior on horseback; second half of 7th century. While the origin of the hoard is still a matter of dispute, stylistic evidence points towards East Anglian booty taken by a Mercian army. (Photo courtesy Archaeology Data Service, ADS)

Reconstruction of helmet from the 7th-century Staffordshire Hoard. Painstakingly reconstructed from fragments by the Dept of Conservation, Birmingham Museum, it is described as 'a magnificent thing', redolent of the authority of the man who wore it. Iconography shows that helmets were sometimes crested; the crest reconstructed here echoes one depicted on the Norbury Stone, where the helmet may represent a later development of the Sutton Hoo type. (Photo courtesy Wikimedia Commons)

are evidence of a Christian presence among the original owners of the treasure – which extended on to the battlefield, it seems. The hoard has thrown new light on the political turmoil of those times, and the materials in the hoard illuminate aspects of Anglo-Saxon military history at just that point when chiefdoms were becoming kingdoms and Christianity was gaining a firm foothold. This was a very turbulent period, in which old power structures were challenged and overthrown as new ones arose.

The hoard was deposited, perhaps in a bag, in a hole dug in open heathland close to the Mercian cathedral city of Lichfield, and not far from the route of the strategic Watling Street (the modern A5). A case can be made for linking the deposit to any of several events in the later 7th century – the aftermath of King Penda's death in 655, for example, or an uprising of 658, or an outbreak of plague in 664. Any of these momentous events might have prompted the owner of the treasure to hide it in a safe place in the vain hope that he could later return to collect it.

Who might have owned the treasure? Its exclusively military nature suggests strongly that it should be seen as victors' plunder from a battlefield. But these gold and bejewelled fittings clearly were not taken to a place of safety for recycling by Mercian goldsmiths and armourers based in Lichfield or Tamworth. Rather, the whole collection appears to have been hastily hidden in a pit out in the countryside where nobody would ever look for it. Was this a desperate attempt at concealment – or was it a pre-Christian deposition ritual intended to put the weapons beyond use?

The question of the hoard's origin has been carefully considered. If it represents battlefield booty, then the likelihood must be that it was taken by the victorious local Mercians from invaders, or during an expedition into neighbouring territory. Examination and comparison do not support the idea of local manufacture, added to which the Christian nature of some items (Mercia was still heathen at this time), and the destructive dismantling of weapon-parts, both suggest that the objects were not Mercian in manufacture or possession. An origin in East Anglia is most likely on historical grounds (there was endemic warfare between the two kingdoms in the mid 7th century), and is supported by the quality of the known output of East Anglian workshops.

The most informative aspect of the find is the quantity of sword pommel caps – of which there appear to be 74 complete examples plus some fragments, totalling 86 in all. The majority are made of gold, with a few silver and gilded copper-alloy examples. They are almost all of very high quality – similar in many respects to the Sutton Hoo Mound 1 sword – and they feature either garnet cloisonné decoration (17 examples) or filigree and granulation (47). The decorative tradition is overwhelmingly in Salin's Style II (1904, r/p 1935), with a few exceptions in the older Style I. This dates the manufacture of the bulk of the hoard to the range $c.575$–$c.650$. Some of the pommels show signs of wear through prolonged use, so a date of deposition between 650 and 675 seems most likely. Since the pommel caps and other items are apparently close in date, they probably represent fittings from the high-status swords of a single force. Furthermore, with so many ornate swords present in a single troop, these must be the remains of the weapons used by the elite, men of either *cyning* or *drihten* (king or warlord) rank or their immediate entourage and champions.

Implications for army size

There were thus in one army at least 86 swords used by men of elite status. Each of these leaders would have led a troop of warriors numbering perhaps no less than ten, and very probably many more if we include the rank-and-file spearmen, subordinate thanes and their supporters. This very fact has implications for the size of the army represented by the hoard.

The ASC (MS A, s.a.784) describes the unsuccessful bid for power in Wessex by a prince named Cyneheard in these terms: 'Here Cyneheard slew King Cynewulf and he was slain there, and 84 men with him.' So it appears that a group of around 100 men (or rather more) supported Cyneheard's bid for power, and that they were a credible force – they had slain Cynewulf, the previous king, but lost their lives in the battle. Cyneheard was not a king but an *æðeling*, probably an *ealdorman* and landowner in his own right. If each *ealdorman* had a force of similar size (100+), equipped with fine weapons which displayed their status, then swords of this type must have been available in some quantity.

It has been calculated that there might be four *ealdormen* at any one time in a large kingdom such as Mercia, each of them with the wealth to

Fragmentary plaques identified as items 596 and 597 from the 7th-century Staffordshire Hoard represent marching warriors with sturdy spears and small round shields. The embossed figures at left and right both wear knee-length ringmail hauberks, while the central figure shows a cross-hatched pattern strongly suggesting quilted 'soft armour'. The left-hand helmet has an eagle *protome*, and the central one shows a ribbed effect; both have attached cheek-guards. (Photo courtesy Archaeology Data Service, ADS)

support a retinue of around 100 thanes, so there could have been 300–400 similar swords in use in the mid-7th century in that kingdom alone. If the swords of the elite warriors represent only the highest ranks, as their rarity in the archaeological record suggests, then they probably account for less than 10 per cent of the total numbers in the field (i.e. for every chief with a gold-hilted sword there are 9 or more men of lower ranks, from thane to spearman). Therefore 400 leaders with gold-hilted swords represent around 4,000 fighting men. Anglo-Saxon armies might thus have comprised several thousands of combatants, as well as all the support staff.

This suggestion has a bearing on the sizes of the forces ranged against them, such as the following in the ASC (MS A, s.a. 837): 'Here Ealdorman Wulfheard fought at Southampton against 33 shiploads [of Danes] and made great slaughter there and took victory'. The stated sizes of Viking armies have often been regarded as exaggerations, due to a supposed tendency to overestimate the numbers of enemy forces. An attack by 33 Danish ships implies a force of around 1,500 men (assuming about 50 men per ship). If Wulfheard, who was just an *ealdorman*, arrived with a personal retinue of 100 elite warriors and their followers, supplemented by the garrison at Southampton, he could have fielded a force of a similar size.

We might alternatively suppose that swords of the quality present in the Staffordshire Hoard were actually very rare, only available to men of the *ealdorman – æþeling – cyning* class, in which case they would represent a proportion closer to 1 per cent of the total present. This would mean that Anglo-Saxon armies might have been even larger, and that the 86 swords in the hoard represent a force closer to 10,000 men. The logistics of moving, feeding, supplying and commanding such large numbers seem daunting, but successful kings attracted successful followers, and it may be that such large military assemblies were sometimes able to take to the field.

C

KING RÆDWALD OF EAST ANGLIA, c.AD 616

(1) King Rædwald

Here we imagine the king welcoming the exiled Edwin of Northumbria to his kingdom on his arrival via the river Deben. The king is depicted with equipment from Mound 1 at Sutton Hoo, and horse harness from Mound 17. He wears the famous helmet from the burial, which bears religious iconography (riders assisted by supernatural figures, warriors dancing with swords and spears, boars' heads on the eyebrows, a serpent on the crest, and a bird on the faceplate), which marks him out as a devotee of his legendary 'ancestor' Woden. Over an *alba*-white tunic with richly decorated gold-on-red bands at the cuffs and hem, his mailcoat has narrow copper decorative edging. Over his ringmail he wears a soft leather 'cuirass' fashioned as a Roman *lorica*, fastened at the shoulders with golden clasps bearing garnet and glass cloisonné ornament including the figures of boars. His sword is slung at his hip in a scabbard worn on a leather belt with gold and garnet cloisonné panels. A heavy, shaggy cloak or mantle rests on his shoulders.

(2) Prince Eorpwald

Eorpwald, Rædwald's eldest son, is partly reconstructed with items from the unidentified young male burial in Mound 17. Tight trousers and leg-bindings were probably preferred when riding a horse, as shown on the Bradwell figurine. The shield is shown in 7th-century Anglo-Saxon art on the helmet plates from Sutton Hoo and in the Staffordshire Hoard iconography; it was probably of modest size, suited to the role of a skirmisher using throwing-spears and/or a bow. The silver-gilt mounts from two large drinking horns were found at Sutton Hoo.

(3) Edwin of Northumbria

Still personally wealthy, Edwin is now an exile arriving at Rædwald's court with limited power and agency. He sports a trimmed moustache and hair cut to collar-length. His long-sleeved yellow linen tunic is obscured by the thick woollen cross-over 'riding coat' with a gold-braid border and lower hem, reconstructed from the Taplow barrow find in Buckinghamshire. The waist is gathered by a broad leather belt with a gilded copper-alloy triangular double fastener with triple bosses, also based on the Taplow finds (Hines & Bayliss Type BU3-d). Close-fitting woollen trousers are confined by crossed leather bindings each ending in a small buckle. He holds a personal *tufa* military standard as described by Bede, and based on evidence from the Welbeck Hill barrow, Lincolnshire – a painted spear with a tuft or tufts of horsehair.

EQUIPMENT & WEAPONS

The survival of organic materials from the Anglo-Saxon period is rare, unless the object has been preserved in either very dry conditions (e.g. a saint's tomb) or very wet (e.g. a boggy deposit). In what follows, it must always be borne in mind that leather, wood, horn and other materials may have been used extensively without leaving any trace in the records. Wood and leather only survive in waterlogged conditions and are rarely found except in small fragments, adhering to metal objects and preserved by their corrosion products.

DEFENSIVE EQUIPMENT:

Helmets

A splendid helmet (OE *cynehelm*) was the battlefield distinction of a leader in the early period. A few examples are known from archaeological discoveries, but may represent only random survivals from the larger numbers which must have been in use. Apart from the archaeology, important information is also presented in the conservative medium of poetry, such as in the 7th–8th century *Beowulf*, whose description of spectacular battle equipment (*heaðowæda*) is confirmed by archaeology. The iron-plate helmet (*wírumbewunden*, 'wound about with wires') comprised a bowl (*héafodbeorge*) and a crest (*wala*) and sometimes a face-plate (*heregrima*). The gilded copper-alloy sheet mountings and plaques were richly embossed with images of mythical warriors and battles. According to the poem, the areas above the cheek-guards of the hero's helmet were ornamented with images of boars, a detail confirmed by archaeology.

Reconstruction of a *spangenhelm*-type helmet, from a find at Vézeronce, France dated to AD 450–500. (Netherlands National Military Museum, Deft; photo courtesy the Curator, Jeroen Punt)

Sutton Hoo, Mound 1 (Suffolk) A classic enclosed iron helmet with silvered plates attached to the outer surface, loosely based on Roman mask helmets, including the face-plate with stylized facial detailing. Preciously decorated mask-helmets (*grímhelmas*) were the result of a long development starting during the Late Roman era. (Helmets like the Vendel XIV example, with its heavy cheek- and neck-guards, were probably modified versions of the Sassanian-inspired or pseudo-Attic Roman cataphract helmets of the period.) The details of the Sutton Hoo helmet indicate a strong association with the Anglian god of war, Woden. Its decoration is in Style II – a common North Sea Germanic format – which led early investigators to conclude that it was probably of Swedish workmanship, since its closest known parallels were helmets found at Valsgärde and Vendel, Sweden. However,

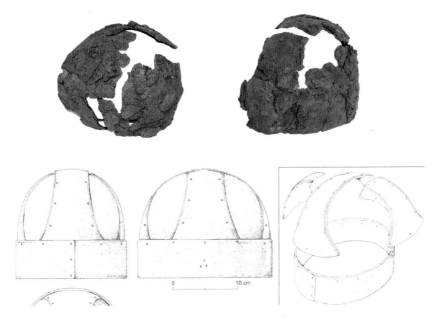

further investigation into differences in the construction techniques indicates its English origin.

The skull is made from a sheet of iron, to the rim of which are attached the deep, movable side-pieces and neck-plate, and a fixed face-plate. Comparable Scandinavian examples are made from iron strips and have hanging iron bars or mail at the rim, not the deep cheek-guards of this and the Wollaston and Coppergate examples. The surface of the skull, neck-plate and side-pieces was covered in decorated copper-alloy foils, each tinned to give a lustrous silvery sheen in discrete zones: the 'rider' motif on the skull, 'dancing warriors' on the brow and side-pieces, and 'interlaced serpents' on the neck-plate and in bands on all these surfaces. The tinned plates are

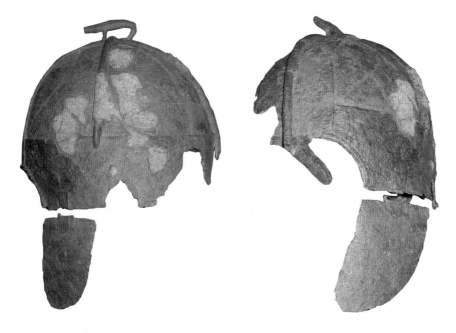

Right side and three-quarter front images of the magnificent 8th-century Coppergate helmet found in York. Note the gilded copper-alloy decorative bands and nasal guard. A ringmail curtain (*aventail* in O.E., *freawrosn*) is suspended by copper-alloy rings which pass through slots cut through the browband, to a wire running around inside the helmet. (Yorkshire Museum, inv. no. YORCM: CA665; photo courtesy Wikimedia Commons)

Three angles of the 10th-century Yarm helmet; found in the North Riding of Yorkshire, this is the first relatively complete Anglo-Scandinavian helmet found in Britain, and only the second Viking helmet discovered in north-west Europe. The iron bowl is made of bands and plates riveted together, with a simple knob at the apex. Below the brow band it has a 'spectacles' guard around the eyes and nose forming a half-mask, which suggests an affinity with earlier Vendel-culture helmets from Sweden. The lower edge of the brow band is pierced with circular holes where a mail *aventail* may have been attached. (Preston Park Museum, Stockton-on-Tees; photos courtesy of Matt Bunker)

held in place by corrugated copper-alloy strips, and the edges of the helmet's various components are finished with U-section guttering. The 'face' sports a neat moustache, prominent nose and eyebrows which combine to form the image of a bird in flight. The crest across the top of the helmet is formed as a snake with a head at each end – a motif found elsewhere in Germanic art. The eyebrows are set with a row of garnets along the lower edge.

Benty Grange (Derbyshire) An iron frame recovered from a burial mound has horn plates forming the skull, and possibly metal foil *pressblech* plates over this. The helmet is surmounted by the figure of a boar, a feature which appears in contemporary iconography but which is seldom found *in situ*. Another barrow nearby at Newhaven House may have held a second similar helmet, unearthed in the 19th century, but what became of it is not known.

Wollaston (Northamptonshire) An iron bowl with reinforcing straps, cheek-plates, and a crest including a stylized boar figure. The style is strikingly similar to helmets worn by horsemen on the 'Aberlemno Stone' in Scotland,

leading some scholars to conclude that the imagery of that monument commemorates an Anglian (Northumbrian) incursion into Pictland.

Shorwell (Isle of Wight) Iron fragments recovered from a grave belong to a *bandhelm* helmet, a simple but effective form not otherwise known to have been in use in Britain. However, some possibly Late Roman fragments found in Dumfriesshire in the 19th century may also have formed part of a similar specimen, but in the shape of a *spangenhelm*.

York (Yorkshire) The Coppergate helmet was found during excavations in the city, deposited in a well. It dates from the later 8th century and is similar in profile to the Wollaston helmet, but is more richly appointed. It has a ringmail *aventail* attached through the lower rim, longer hinged cheek-plates, and a long nasal with decorated edges to the eyes terminating in beast-heads. The gilded strips which form a cross on the bowl are inscribed with a text in large, decorative insular capitals: *IN. NOMINE. DNI. NOSTRI IHV. SCS. SPS. D. ET. OMNIBUS DECEMUS. AMEN. OSHERE. XPI.* ('In the name of our Lord Jesus, the Holy Spirit, God and all, we pray. Amen. Oshere. Christ.') 'Oshere' is presumed to be the name of the owner; many Northumbrian kings had names beginning with '*os-*' (e.g. Osric, Oswine, Oswulf), which means 'heathen god'. It is likely enough that this Oshere was a (junior?) member of the royal family; how his fabulous helmet came to be hidden in the shaft of a well is still a mystery.

Yarm (Northumberland) A rather poor-quality helmet found at this village was for years regarded as a modern copy imitating a Viking style of helmet (e.g. the find from Gjermundbu, Norway). Recent (2020) re-examination indicates that the metal and details of construction are actually consistent with a possibly 10th-century date, and the Yarm helmet must therefore be considered 'probably genuine'. It is thus only the second (after Gjermendbu) intact Viking-period helmet found in north-west Europe. A recent interpretation by T. Vlasaty suggests an even earlier dating, i.e. 6th–9th century, due to its possible affinity with the Swedish helmets from Uppland (Vendel, Valsgärde), but the Yarm helmet is still firmly classified as 10th-century by the York archaeologists.

In addition, there are several fragmentary helmets, most notably the various parts (crest, cheek-guards, etc.) included in the 7th-century Staffordshire Hoard. A repoussé *pressblech* foil recovered from a burial mound at Caenby (Lincolnshire) probably belonged to a rich helmet, possibly similar to the Sutton Hoo example.

Simple conical helmets are visible in 11th-century manuscripts, often rendered in shades of blue probably symbolizing iron. Alongside these iron examples, head protections made partially or entirely from boiled and moulded leather (*cuir bouilli*) were probably widely used, but do not survive. If such headgear were dyed (yellow in the Cotton MS Claudius IV – called hereinafter the *Hexateuch* – folio 25r), if painted or otherwise

The 8th-century 'Repton Stone', probably representing a mounted Anglian leader in full armour. He clearly sports a large moustache, and seems to wear on his head a circlet with filigree decoration. In his left hand is a shield, and at his waist an unmistakable Type III *seax*, perhaps 45cm/18ins long, and characteristically worn horizontally. The mouth of the sheath may have metal reinforcement, since rivets are visible, along with a 'V'-shape. His main protection is a scale armour, as explained in the text. His thighs are covered by the folds of a knee-length tunic, of which the carved detail rules out interpretation as Roman-style *pteryges*. He wears *winingas* – cloth 'puttees' – on his lower legs. (Derby Archaeological Museum; photo Raffaele D'Amato, courtesy of the Museum)

ornamented, it would still have made an impressive display despite its functional limitations. This is a possible explanation for the 'Phrygian' crenelated caps worn in battle in the miniatures of the *Hexateuch* and other manuscripts.

Armour

Literary sources tell us that body armour normally took the form of a mailcoat. One Old English riddle (*Exeter Book*, riddle 35) specifically describes such a garment, in terms which indicate that it was a familiar item. The *Beowulf* poet (7th–8th century) likewise refers to mailcoats by a number of different words (*byrnie, gúðbyrne, searonet*, etc), which indicate that his audience was expected to be acquainted with such armour. The body armour in the poem is mainly recorded as a shining war-coat made of iron rings (*hringírenscír*), often gilded and decorated (*fratwa gelaéded*). This type of body armour already existed in Scandinavia during the early Iron Age, imported from the Celtic tribes of Central Europe. The decoration of such armour had Eastern origins, and at the time of chieftains like *Beowulf* was mainly reserved to leaders and limited numbers of their high-ranking retainers.

Sculpture from the shaft of the 'Brailsford Cross', representing a 9th-century warrior. The prominent sword and small raised shield suggest a member of the Anglo-Scandinavian elite, but this identification is speculative. He seems to be dressed in a similar fashion to the warrior on the Repton Stone, which predates the Viking occupation of that area. (*in situ*, All Saints' Church, Brailsford, Derbyshire; photo Raffaele D'Amato, courtesy of the parish)

Lawcodes dating from the 10th century require men presenting themselves for military service to be equipped with a mailcoat, and the *Anglo-Saxon Chronicle* records a royal decree which is translated thus: 'Here the king ordered that across all the English nation ships must be made constantly, that is then from every 310 hides one *scegð* [light warship] and from every eight hides a helmet and mailcoat'.

The surviving physical evidence is far from re-assuring, however: the only known Anglo-Saxon example of a ringmail coat is the tangled ferrous mass recovered from Mound 1 at Sutton Hoo. Carefully restored and reconstructed, this appears to have been thigh-length, with small (8mm) iron rings linked four-in-one forming the main protection, and copper-alloy links at the edges.

Mail armour is also represented in art, but its interpretation is not always clear. The miniature of folio 24v in the *Hexateuch* represents Abraham as a king wearing a short-sleeved mail hauberk rendered as if made from large rings. Is this a realistic representation of a typical 11th-century mailcoat, or something else? The iconography (see page 18) might represent a *broigne annelée*, i.e. a leather coat covered by juxtaposed or superimposed iron rings placed row-by-row and stitched onto the leather backing. This thesis, which is supported by Charles Hamilton Smith and Viollet le Duc when referring to some of the armour represented on the Bayeux Tapestry, has long been contested, but cannot be dismissed out of hand. Its existence might be argued from the rarity of any complete mail armour made of interlaced rings. At the end of the 7th century a verse by Bishop Aldhelm (*Aenigmata Aldhelmi IV,* 3) might suggest that armour made only of interlaced iron rings was rare compared to the more usual *broigne.*

A carved cross-shaft from the church of St Mary Bishophill Junior, York, dated on stylistic grounds to *c.*AD 850, around the time when Saxon Northumbria was fighting for its existence against the Danes. The stone, measuring 66cm/25.9ins high, shows two figures. The left-hand man is shown in profile, wearing a hood or *coif,* a knee-length padded (?) coat, and with a horn attached to his waist belt. The right-hand figure is bare-headed, wears a long belted garment with a raised collar, and holds the hilt of his apparently Anglo-Saxon sword at his waist. The interlaced detail under their feet is too worn for identification of the original subject. This monument has sometimes been assumed to be Anglo-Scandinavian, but the carving is consistent with the local Anglian tradition. (Yorkshire Museum, accession no. YORYM: 1979.53)

Certainly the fact that on folio 24v the only man armoured is the king, Abraham, suggests that ringmail was reserved to the elite.

Another possibility is that the armour represented in the miniature is composed of small or medium-sized scales. This type of armour was used by the Anglo-Saxon elite, being well represented on the 8th-century Repton Stone, where the warlord (a probable member of the Mercian royal house, perhaps even King Æþelbald himself) is clearly wearing a *squama* over an under-armour garment showing from the waist down. These scales are also represented (also with an under-garment, very similarly arranged) on the famous Franks Casket.

There is discussion among scholars as to whether these two monuments represent mail or scale armour, but bearing in mind the contemporary Frankish iconography (especially the *Stuttgart Psalter*) the answer is more probably scale. On the Repton Stone this does not appear to cover the upper thighs, which are protected by the padded under-corselet. A recent (2000) work of scholarship comments that the Repton Stone shows 'a mounted warrior wearing a mail shirt'. Although sketches of the carving make the texture appear to show circles, close examination of the actual carving reveals that the elements are off-circular, with downwards overlapping and 'shingling' typical of scale armour. While it does not extend below the torso, it does onto the upper arms, like the scale armour of Late Roman soldiers in the early 4th-century sculpture in the Vatican Museum, section Chiaramonti.

Armours of iron scale and *lamellae* were certainly in use in continental Europe at the time of the Repton Stone. While we can only theorize as to what such a cuirass might have been called in Old English, it too might have been termed a *byrnie*. The word '*byrne*' is of unknown origin, but some derive it from *brūn* ('burnished, shining'), and the scale cuirass would certainly have qualified for that description, especially if the scales had been dipped in molten tin. We might guess that the Anglo-Saxons might have called this harness a '*scealu-byrne*' or perhaps a '*wyrmfell byrne*' ('dragon-skin armour').

Other than metallic armour, padded garments foreshadowing the later medieval *gambeson* were worn – either providing an under-layer for a mailcoat, or worn alone. The latter seems to be the case for some soldiers on the Franks Casket, whose striped garments are not simply tunics, but imitate the Late Antique *thoracomaci* or *subarmales* fitted with hanging strips like *pteryges*. Here, however, the garment's stripes are compact and give the impression of being sewn together, as in the medieval *gambeson*, and as also visible in

A 6th-century iron shield boss with silver and gold fittings, from Mucking, Essex. (British Museum; photo Raffaele D'Amato, courtesy of the Museum)

contemporary Frankish iconography (*Stuttgart Psalter*, folio 52; *Arator Subdiaconus, Historia Apostolica*, folio 54v). Quilted leather and cloth garments as alternatives to metal armours could have been produced easily and inexpensively using the technologies of the period.

A fragmentary carved stone cross at the church of St Mary Bishophill in York shows two standing figures, each with an impressive moustache (see photo opposite). The figure on the left has a cloak or mantle thrown over what may be some form of armour on his shoulders, a hood (or helmet?), a broad waist belt, and a horn slung at his hip. He appears to be restraining the figure on the right, who also wears a mantle over a collared garment. Both men wear outer garments with a carefully carved quilted texture suggestive of padded armour, such as is also visible on 7th-century plaques found at Sutton Hoo and in the Staffordshire Hoard. It is equally plausible that metal reinforcement plates might have been sewn into the body of such garments, as in the much later 'coat of plates'. The warrior on the 9th-century Norbury Stone (see page 6) seems to wear padded armour perhaps reinforced with metallic discs.

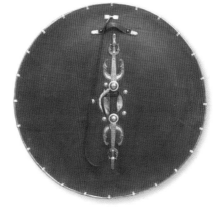

Reconstruction of the outer and inner faces of the 7th-century shield from Sutton Hoo, Mound 1. The gilded copper-alloy mounts on the outside represent a dragon and a bird. (ex Pollington, Kerr & Hammond, 2010; Mortimer Collection)

Both sides of a 5th-century war axe of Frankish type; it shows various affinities with finds on the continent, and in England (at Howletts, Kent). According to Harrison (1993), it has a Merovingian origin, of a type normally used by cavalry. (Lewes Museum, Alfriston, E. Sussex; photo courtesy of Matt Bunker)

Shields

The shield was conventionally a wooden disc of several boards laid edge-to-edge, the most commonly-used woods being poplar (*populus*) or willow (*salix*). Shields were probably finely crafted from thin laths curved into a lenticular form and tapered towards the outer edge. The inner and outer faces were covered with leather (Prittlewell grave 121) – a law of King Cnut forbids the use of sheepskin for this purpose. A protruding metal boss covered a central cut-out over the internal handgrip, and various metal mountings – simultaneously decorative and protective – were occasionally fitted, as was metal edge-binding. The poem *Beowulf* describes leather-covered shields made of wood, richly ornamented with metal ribs and fitted with bosses, strengthened with metal around the edges (*rondas regnhearde, faéttes cyldas*).

Three views of a complete and well-preserved Anglo-Danish asymmetric iron axehead from the 10th or 11th century. Weapons of this type are typically known as 'Dane axes', and are depicted on the Bayeux Tapestry being wielded two-handed by the English, particularly the housecarls. The haft-socket is of D-section, and has triangular projections pointing both up and down the haft. This axe is similar to R.E.M. Wheeler's Type VI (1927), which he dates to around AD 1000 onward, referring to 15 examples from the Thames and several from the Home Counties and southern East Anglia. A number of similar axes, found at the northern end of old London Bridge, are now in the Museum of London collection. (PAS record BUC-B7ACE2, licence CC BY-SA 4.0)

The shield bosses of the elite were often of the common domed typology, but there are important exceptions. The boss might be strengthened by a central protrusion or spike and studs, usually flat, although this form later gave way to simpler domed profiles. The magnificent shield recovered from Mound 1 at Sutton Hoo featured gilded copper-alloy panels around its boss, of which the central stud was topped with a gilt-copper disc with inset garnets. Unusually, this shield featured almost as much decoration on the reverse as on the front, with gilded vertical bars developing into pairs of beast-heads, and paired fixtures at the rim – perhaps to attach a slinging strap. The handgrip was of wood reinforced with iron and bound with leather.

The size of the boards can seldom be determined. Iconography (e.g. the Bradwell figurine) often shows shields as quite small, covering the bent arm from shoulder to hand, so e.g. 45–65cm/18–25ins in diameter. Early grave finds indicate that the face of the shield was decorated with metal studs, plates and other fittings ornamented with animal, fish, bird and other motifs. The majestic example from Sutton Hoo Mound 1 was much larger – the metal rim showing a diameter of 93cm/36.6ins – and decorated with metal plates formed as a bird and a dragon. Iconography and archaeology indicate that throughout the Anglo-Saxon period shields were usually circular and either flat or convex, but during the 11th century the longer 'teardrop' or 'kite'-shaped shield was introduced, probably under influence from the East. The Bayeux Tapestry also shows one warrior using a rectangular shield with rounded corners, an archeologically confirmed design that has echoes in the art of Ireland and Pictish Scotland.

In *Beowulf* the shields had a yellow rim or were painted yellow. Designs for shield blazons are known from 11th century sources, especially from the *Hexateuch* (foliate decoration) and from the Bayeux Tapestry. Some miniatures from the Cotton MS Claudius show broad shields whose surface is divided by radial bands, which in some cases are reinforced by studs or nails (folio 24v), and in others are marked by blue or red lines (folio 25v). These radial bands, probably derived from those decorating Carolingian and Ottonian shields, seem to be typical of royal bodyguards (folio 34r). Again, the surface of the royal shields in that manuscript is painted plain yellow (folio 25), or sometimes only around the rim, suggesting metal edging. Shield bosses were still in use in the 11th century, and in the Cotton MS Claudius are represented as conical, painted black, light blue or reddish-mauve.

WEAPONS:

Axes
Axes feature widely in the early Anglo-Saxon period in the form of the light *francisca* throwing-axe, with its curved head and swept blade. Surviving examples are seldom decorated, and it may be that these missile weapons were regarded as expendable. Nevertheless, the hafts may have been carved or painted, if only for identification.

Axes of conventional design were important to Anglo-Saxon warriors, sometimes having a status similar to that of the sword, and were carried by the same elite class. They were representative of wealth and privilege, and were often included as grave goods, such as the Alfriston axe from Sussex.

A long axe-hammer with an iron haft and head, the blade angled downwards, and with a complex swivel-ring at the end of the haft, was found in Mound I at Sutton Hoo. This was probably not a weapon of war but rather a ceremonial piece, probably used for the public slaughter of cattle and horses for ritual feasting. Iconographic evidence (e.g. the Bayeux

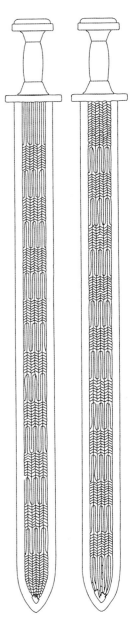

Reconstruction of the Acklam Wold sword from North Yorkshire, which has been variously dated. The pattern-welded blade was made from 12 composite rods, and the hilt shows traces of ivory and gold filigree, with a wire-inlaid pommel. (Drawing by Andrea Salimbeti, ex Ben Mortimer, 2019)

Reconstruction of the sword hilt and scabbard fittings from Mound 1 at Sutton Hoo, plus a suspended sword bead from Dover (Buckland, grave 93); first half of 7th century. The two short suspension straps associated with the two domed gilt cloisonné bosses probably allowed the scabbard to be removed without unfastening the waist belt. (ex Pollington, Kerr & Hammond, 2010; Mortimer Collection)

Tapestry) shows 10th- to 11th-century warriors with large, two-handed axes. These are probably the weapons called in Norse *skeggøx* ('beard-axe'), presumably from their asymmetric blade shape, and were associated with the *húskarlar*.

Swords

The sword (Latin, *ensis, spatha*; Old English, *sweord, mece*) was the most symbolically important weapon of the Anglo-Saxon elite. Though the spear was more widely used, the sword had a prestige and glamour greater than that of any other weapon.

The typology of hilt parts (pommel, grip and guard) has been studied for nearly two centuries, and several classification systems have been devised. These tie the early (5th- to 8th-century) evidence to developments in France and the Rhineland, while later types share characteristics with Scandinavian finds. Given that so-called 'Viking' blades generally originated in the Rhineland and were fitted with hilts and scabbards locally, the similarity of Anglo-Saxon, Frankish and later Scandinavian finds is hardly surprising.

It has been estimated that swords are found with about one burial in 20 (5 per cent of graves) in Anglo-Saxon cemeteries. Such a figure should not be taken at face value, since we cannot know how representative of society at large these furnished burials really are – while study of the many cremation cemeteries seldom produces any evidence for swords at all. That said, it may be supposed that swords were not available to everybody, and that ownership of one conferred some status. This is confirmed by the highly decorated

Pommel and part of grip from the Fetter Lane sword, late 8th century. This impressive piece was made of silver with gilt and niello decoration on an organic base, and the main panels of the grip are decorated on both sides with animal and foliate motifs. (British Museum; photo Raffaele D'Amato, courtesy of the Museum)

elements of many hilts, like the specimen found in Mixnam's Pit, Chertsey, with a copper-inlaid hilt, and another find from Cumberland of a profiled hilt in wood and horn with indented gold elements. On the other hand, more than 80 mostly high-status sword pommels were found in the Staffordshire Hoard alone, showing that swords were more numerous than previously thought. In the early centuries elite swords often had attached to the hilt a dangling sword-bead made of glass, amber or perhaps horn.

An important category of 6th- to 7th-century swords had

the pommel decorated with a ring, as also present on the contemporary swords of other Germanic peoples such as the Lombards. According to Evison (1956), interlinked rings symbolized a bond of mutual loyalty between lord and warrior. One suggestion is that the ring meant that the sword was given by a leader to a thane as a reward for service or a symbol of elite rank. The ring-hilted sword has elsewhere been linked to the practice of ritual oath-taking.

Ring-hilted swords are a feature mainly of finds in Kent and elsewhere in the south-east from the 6th and 7th centuries, and this characteristic style of hilt fitting is termed the 'Bifrons-Gilton pommel type', from early find sites in Kent. It suggests that Kentish kings were influenced by contemporary Merovingian Frankish customs during a period of Frankish hegemony usually ascribed to c.520–570, a period of consolidation when chiefdoms were developing around a few powerful kinship groups. Identical customs are found in Kentish cemeteries such as Ash Gilton and Faversham, and Frankish ones such as St Dizier. The contemporary finds of ring-pommels in Västergotland (Sweden) and Westphalia (Germany) may be considered as outliers of this cultural group.

The blades of early swords were made by the pattern-welding technique, whereby several grades of iron bars were welded together alternating in twisted and straight sections to produce a stratified linear effect; this could be etched

RIGHT

Anglo-Saxon iron *seax* with silvered copper-alloy 'cocked-hat' pommel and fittings; 7th-8th century, from Oliver's Battery, Winchester, Hampshire; total length, 39.3cm/15.4 inches. When it was excavated, iron corrosion could be seen to preserve the remains of a wooden sheath, probably of oak. (Winchester City Museum, photo courtesy of Matt Bunker)

FAR RIGHT

The 10th-century 'Beagnoth' or Battersea *seax*, with a 72cm/28.4-in blade with the back running almost parallel to the straight cutting edge before being angled towards the point. The broad tang is offset sideways from the centre of the blade, which is decorated on both faces with linear ornament formed by hammering polychrome wires into the surface of the metal, including a Runic alphabet and the name of either the smith or the owner. (British Museum, inv. no. 1857,0623.1; photo courtesy of Wikimedia Commons)

and ground to reveal 'star' patterns and other effects. Pattern-welded blades were certainly the prerogative of elite warriors. We find them in great number in the pre-Christian graves (e.g. in Prittlewell grave 121, accompanied by a beechwood scabbard covered in textile and lined with fleece).

The typical sword of the early period (e.g. that from Mound 1 at Sutton Hoo) does not appear to have featured a fuller, although this was present on blades from the 9th century onward. The pommels represented on the Cotton IV BL manuscript are round or three-lobed in shape (folio 25v), which links them with Petersen's Type S (folio 38r) or X (folio 36v), like the example held by Harold when taken captive in the Bayeux Tapestry.

The scabbard was formed as two wooden laths (usually radially cut or split, and 2cm/0.78in thick) held in a leather casing with metal fittings at the mouth and lower end (chape). The form and decoration of these fittings allows a systematic dating and typology to be proposed. In some cases it is likely that foundation moulding (a carved wooden core with leather shrunk tight over it) was used to produce a decorative design in raised ribs across the surface; this

---

E   **'OFFA's DYKE', LATE 8th CENTURY AD**

(1) King Offa of Mercia

Offa is credited with ordering the construction of this impressive earthwork along the border between Mercia and the hostile Welsh kingdom of Powys. We reconstruct the king's appearance as in his vigorous middle age, and his costume partly from the carvings on the Franks Casket. He wears a crimson 'Phrygian' cap, and a knee-length tunic. This shows pleats below the waist; hints of transverse folds on the forearm; gold brocade edging, including bands from the collar down the vent on the chest; and note a gold left arm-ring. His tight-fitting linen trousers are confined with tapes, each with a silver-gilt hooked tag fastening just below the knee, and he wears calf-length leather boots of Carolingian style. His short mantle in rich green silk is decorated with a repeat pattern, and is fastened at his right shoulder with a silver-gilt disc brooch. Slung from a leather belt with a long hanging strap-end is his scabbarded sword with a silver-gilt hilt, copied from the Fetter Lane specimen. (see photo, page 34)

(2) King Beorhtric of Wessex

To Offa's left side stands his younger ally Beorhtric. He wears a blue cloak hanging open at the front to below his knees, copied from the Franks Casket; its silver disc brooch with small raised bosses is from the Evington specimen. His rich saffron-yellow tunic is, again, pleated below the waist. He holds a sword with a silver and gilt pommel, from a specimen found at Chiswick on the river Thames.

(3) West Saxon warlord

Between and behind the two kings, a warlord stands in attendance on Beorhtric. His helmet is a composite of the Coppergate and Wollaston specimens, in comparison with the Franks Casket. He is protected by a knee-length leather coat quilted with diamond-pattern stitching copied from the St John's Bishopshill Cross, and a high collar. The bindings of his trousers would again have small silver fastening tags. His sword has a silver pommel with inlaid gilt panels (from the Windsor specimen), and at his feet is a shield with a 'sugarloaf' boss (from British Museum specimen 1912, 1220.3). On campaign, he carries a finely mounted drinking horn as a sign of status.

A shorter so-called 'broken-back' 9th- or 10th-century *seax* from Sittingbourne in Kent. It is inscribed in insular majuscules ✠*BIORHTELM ME ꝒORTE* ('Biorhtelm made me') and on the reverse ✠*S[I]GEBEREHT ME AH* ('S[i]gebereht owns me'). (British Museum; photo courtesy of Matt Bunker)

feature has been detected on scabbards from the bog-deposit at Nydam (Denmark) in the area from which the Angles originated.

Early chapes – such as that from Kingston by Lewes (6th century), or one from Brighthampton – were of copper alloy, often short-armed, broad and with gilding, or long-armed, and both asymmetrical. Decorated specimens were probably related to elite warriors.

The suspension system is well documented in the iconography and archaeology. Sometimes the swords were slung at the waist, either in a near-horizontal position (picture stone from Sockburn, Co Durham) or at a steeper angle to the rear (Sutton Hoo, Sigmund Stone, and Winchester Old Minster). The scabbard could be worn from a baldric (Goliath in MS Cotton Tiberius), or be attached to a waist belt, perhaps by a button passing through a slit in the belt (Harold scabbard on Bayeux Tapestry). Equally, it might have been attached by a looped strap (again, Goliath in MS Cotton Tiberius); in the case of the surviving Gloucester scabbard, such a strap might have passed through two slits in the case. It is interesting to note (*Hexateuch*, folio 38v) that the marching lord is not wearing a sword, but weapons are carried by servants in his baggage train.

The *seax*

The word *seax* or *sax* denotes a single-edged knife, as was in common use by all levels of society for domestic as well as military purposes. Iron knives are a common find in Anglo-Saxon cemeteries, although corrosion usually prevents us from appreciating their original design and fineness of execution. The military knife shares its basic form with the hunting knife from which it derives. The iron blade is usually quite short and very sturdy, with a thick back edge; a scooped point (i.e. a 'Bowie-knife' shape) develops from the 8th century onwards.

The inlaid decoration on the blade may be all that survives to indicate what a magnificent weapon a found *seax* originally was. An example in the British Museum from Sittingbourne, Kent, bears inlaid silver panels and the reserved inscriptions '+*Biorthelm me porte*' and '+*S[i]gebereht me ah*'. Another superb example recovered from the river Thames at Battersea, also in the British Museum, is 72.1cm/28.4ins long without its original hilt, and is inlaid with silver and copper-alloy decoration including a complete runic alphabet (*fuþorc*) and the owner's or maker's name '*Beagnoth*'.

The *seax* was worn in a sheath of leather with a tooled design, of which examples survive from London, Hexham, Lincoln, Durham and York. Sheaths were made from a single piece of leather with one seam, and may have been moulded directly around the blade itself. The basic type was a folded flap of leather, sewn or riveted along its upper edge, with small buckles, and reinforcements at the mouth and point to prevent wear; later sheaths were carefully sewn along the centre of the reverse. A characteristic pattern on early types consists of tooled ribbing following the profile of the blade, while the upper section, which partly covers the hilt, is cross-hatched within a rectangular panel. A few examples bear a maker's formula: '+*BYRHTSIGE MEC F[E]CIÐ*' on one from Aachen, Germany, and '+*EDRIC ME FECI[T]*' i.e. 'Eadric made me' on another from Dublin. It is likely that the names are those of the weaponsmiths rather than the leatherworkers.

Evidence from graves and iconography shows that the weapon was worn across the stomach – probably with the sharp edge uppermost and with the hilt at the right-hand end. This would make withdrawal quicker and easier, and, by preventing the blade from resting on its cutting edge, both the sheath and the edge would have been protected from undue wear. The small buckles may have fastened straps which attached it to the belt.

Small knives for general use, 14cm/5½ins long and with horn handles and leather sheaths, are also recorded from princely graves (e.g. Prittlewell grave 121). One remarkable suite of knives was found at Dover (Buckland cemetery, grave 93), with a large 'cutlass' in a wooden-cored leather sheath flanked by two smaller horn-hilted knives. It may be that this represents a huntsman's group, with the larger blade used for the kill and the smaller ones used for cleaning the carcass.

Spears and javelins

It should be borne in mind that the spear was wielded more often in hunting than in war, and that proficiency in its use was a badge of male achievement. In the 9th century King Alfred calls the male line of family descent the *sperehealf* ('spear-side') while the female is the *spinelhealf* ('spindle-side').

The heavy thrusting spear is the commonest weapon recovered from Anglo-Saxon graves, and also appears frequently in manuscript illustrations and elsewhere. The iron head was usually lozenge-shaped with a slender neck, and a split socket which was nailed to the wooden shaft. Grave finds show that a minority of spears were furnished with a ferrule on the butt. The shaft was often of ash wood *(fraxinus)*, and typically around 2m/6½ft long. A typology of forms has been established for Anglo-Saxon and Scandinavian spearheads, which vary mainly in having either a closed or a split socket, and in the relative broadness of the blade. Decoration is confined to small inlaid geometric and other designs at the base of the blade (e.g. the find from Hollingborough, Kent), and occasionally a gilded copper-alloy band at the socket (e.g. the example from Great Chesterford, Essex, now in the British Museum).

In the late miniatures a type of long spear wielded by kings and their retinues is represented with a barbed head reinforced with two or three transverse 'wings' below (*Hexateuch*, folios 24v & 25r), and the shoulders reinforced by volutes. While usually called today a 'boar-spear', this weapon is often represented in 11th-century battle scenes, which proves that it was not used only for hunting. Interestingly, in the *Hexateuch* manuscript these barbed spearheads alternate with squared blades characterized by a spherical counterweight below the head (folios 39r & 39v), a typology usually visible among East Roman spears of the period.

The spear shaft is usually represented in medium brown, suggesting bare, unpainted wood. While decorated shafts are not well attested archaeologically in Britain, some of the earlier Danish bog-finds featured carved and pigmented panels and occasionally a short runic text, all designed to impress and to personalize the weapon. Some of the shaft fragments recovered from the early 7th-century Prittlewell princely chamber grave in Essex also bear engraved interlace detailing; these were presumably for identification as well as showing off the warrior's taste in decoration.

Javelins or throwing spears (*daroð*) were also used, and the Bayeux Tapestry shows a warrior in the English shieldwall carrying three of these in his left hand behind his shield, while brandishing a fourth in his right hand. An early form is called in the modern literature an *angon*, and features a narrow, sharply barbed head on a short shaft. Javelins might be carried in a purpose-made case or quiver, as attested by the armed figure from the Norbury Stone in Derbyshire and by many manuscript illustrations.

Spearhead from Great Chesterford, Essex, 5th century. This originally magnificent spearhead must have belonged to an elite warrior; it is decorated with inlaid roundels near the shoulder, and a socket-ring bearing zoomorphic decoration in Germanic Style I. (ex Pollington, Kerr & Hammond, image Lindsay Kerr, 2010)

Bows

The use of bows in warfare was mainly confined to lower social ranks, although they were popular with the elite for hunting, and representations of their use in war are visible on the Franks Casket. In the Prittlewell princely burial an arrowhead was found, but the lack of any other archery element makes it more logical to suppose that this was the cause of the buried man's death rather than part of his own war-gear. References to the bow used in war are few: in *The Battle of Maldon* the two sides were able to harm each other only 'through arrow's flight' (*þurhflanesflyht*, line 71), and in the initial stages 'bows were busy' (*bogan wæronbysige*, line 110), while towards the end of the poem Æscferþ's contribution was that 'he sent many arrows speeding forth – sometimes he struck a shield, sometimes wounded a warrior' (lines 269–270). This is probably due to the initially static nature of this combat, when the English and Danes were at first physically separated by a waterway and missiles were the only available choice.

The bow is well represented in the miniatures (e.g. *Hexateuch*, folio 36v), but not in the hands of kings or their followers. One exception is the bow of 'Welsh' type (an ancestor of the longbow) depicted in the hands of Esau in the same manuscript (folio 41v); it is shown as white and the quiver as black, with white-fletched arrows. Esau being an important character in the Old Testament, this might be the representation of a nobleman out hunting.

CLOTHING

Tunics

The main garments of male Anglo-Saxons (*Anglisaxones*) were tunics and trousers, which in the early period were tailored wide and made in linen (Paulus Diaconus, IV, 22). A short-sleeved tunic like the Roman-style one recovered from Thorsberg was probably part of their earlier clothing. According to Paulus Diaconus – if this passage also refers to Anglo-Saxon garments – they were ornamented with broad borders woven in various colours. Physical remains of English garments from the early and middle

Detail of left panel from the 8th-century 'Franks Casket', representing the siege of Jerusalem in AD 70 under the Emperor Titus. The carvings on this Northumbrian whalebone chest show important details of contemporary Anglo-Saxon war gear. The leader of the Romans (centre) wears a 'Phrygian' helmet or cap and advances with a drawn sword, followed by a man in scale armour similar to that on the contemporary Repton Stone. Other soldiers are clad in what seems to be 'muscled' armour, worn over a padded garment, showing vertical folds, to protect the lower abdomen and groin. The Anglo-Saxon military equipment of the Northumbrian elite was widely influenced by Carolingian styles, which, under Italian and Eastern Roman influences, still included pseudo-Roman armours. The realism of the equipment represented on the casket is supported by one of the warriors carved on the lid, who wears a helmet virtually identical to the famous Coppergate find from York. (British Museum; photo Rafaele D'Amato, courtesy of the Museum)

'David slaughtering Goliath', a miniature from the poems of Paulinus of Nola. This illustration includes a rare image of a Benty Grange-type helmet with an animal crest. Note the down-curved guard quillons of the sword, typical of 9th- to 10th-century Anglo-Saxon finds. (St Petersburg Public Library, Ms.Q.v.XIV.I; drawing by Andrea Salimbeti ex Nicolle)

periods are confined to a few mineralized scraps of cloth recovered from graves, and some woven bands placed in the tombs of saints.

The tunic (*cyrtel* or *tunece*) of the later elite, as represented in 11th-century manuscripts (*Hexateuch*, folio 22r, and Bayeux Tapestry) is knee-length and long-sleeved, sometimes with the forearms showing transverse folds. Often the abdomen is shown 'pouching' down over the belt, which it thus conceals. The fullness of the skirt is often indicated, as in sculptures where the skirt is represented longer at the sides than in the middle with a curving hem, as on the Norbury Stone. The tunic sleeve of the archer on an 11th- century ivory cross is slightly flared but other images show smooth, close-fitting sleeves extending to the wrist.

Colours and ornamentation might indicate status. Kings may be represented with red tunics and gold cuffs (probably indicating embroidery with gold thread or silk or gold brocading, e.g. King Edgar in MS Vespasian A VIII). Gold brocade formed part of the costume of the occupant of the 7th-century burial mound at Taplow, Buckinghamshire, but the garment to which

Detail from the rear panel of the Franks Casket. The abandoned Romulus and Remus are found by four hunters, one of them (left) dressed in an elegant vernacular short cloak fastened on the right by a round *fibula*. This man may represent an *ealdorman*, since he shows long tunic sleeves having a pleated appearance like those of noblemen in later manuscripts. The other warriors, symbolizing his retinue, are dressed in tunics having tighter skirts, as indicated by a line beneath the buttocks, and some have plain close-fitting sleeves. (British Museum; photo Raffaele D'Amato, courtesy of the Museum)

it was applied had perished. The brocade appeared to be attached at the collar and to extend down the front of the body as a hem. It is likely that the garment was what some modern commentators have called a 'riding jacket', of a type used widely in northern Europe from the 6th century onwards, with the frontal panels overlapping one over the other.

The scholar Gale R. Owen-Crocker suggests that the royal costume of King Athelstan in the Cambridge Corpus Christi College MS 183 shows a linen tunic (to judge from its light shade), terminating in a decorated cuff or wrist band. The neckline of this tunic is marked by a decorated band placed at the top of the shoulder, indicating an aperture wide enough to pass over the head. In the *Life of Edward* (pp.22–33) we have a reference to earlier Anglian kings: 'It had not been the custom for English kings in bygone days to wear clothes of great splendour, apart from cloaks and robes adorned at the top with gold in the national style'. This suggests that such gold edging was considered normal for kings. Green-blue is often used in the *Hexateuch* for the tunics of kings and their retinues (folio 25r), but red is also visible (folio 38r).

Royal servants seem to have worn similar but simplified tunics, of medium blue or light brown colour. Usually the tunics shown in manuscript illuminations are plain and without decoration, but one worn by an elite guard represented as Goliath (*Tiberius Psalter*, folios 8v & 9r), as well as those of the noblemen (folio 8v), are decorated on the skirts with floral patterns as well as rows of dots and lines, dotted cuffs and necklines. The tunic is often represented with a slit at the front of the neck and a wide collar (*sweor-claþ* or *sweor-sal*) often depicted in contrasting colours or, as in the *Tiberius Psalter*, decorated with dots. Goliath is wearing a tunic with this type of border at the neck, with the additional feature of two strings, ending in tags, with which the neck opening is laced or drawn together. Interestingly, his sleeves, like those of the guardsmen in the Cotton B IV, are marked from elbow to wrist in a series of parallel transverse lines terminating at the wrists in a band which is decorated with dots on gold embroidery (see photo below). It is not clear what these parallel lines are meant to represent – perhaps bracelets or arm-rings awarded for service? But more probably, based on the miniatures of the *Hexateuch* and samples in Late Roman art (e.g. Colossus of Barletta), these are simply transverse folds or ruches in the sleeves.

Belts

These had been associated since antiquity with masculinity and military status. Belts worn prominently by otherwise naked or partly-clad warriors feature in European art back to the Bronze Age. True belt buckles made their

Goliath, also from the Cotton manuscript of c.AD 1050–75. The warrior has an embroidered tunic apparently with transverse-pleated sleeves and a loosely-hanging skirt. Note also that he wears buskins or hose over his trousers. (British Library, MS Tiberius C VI, folio 9r; photo courtesy of the Library)

The 6th-century Bradwell 'gaming piece', found in Norfolk. This copper-alloy figurine is only 37.5mm/1.5ins tall by 42mm/1.6ins long , but is precisely fashioned. Note the bridle and reins, and straps running to the rump and beneath the tail indicating the use of a saddle. The rider has thick, collar-length hair, and sports a narrow moustache. A scabbarded sword is slung at his left hip and extends over the horse's flank. His left hand grips a small circular shield with a central *umbo*, while his right loosely holds the reins. (Private collection, photo courtesy Timeline Auctions)

first appearance in northern Europe with the advent of the Roman armies, replacing a form of cast copper-alloy toggle used to secure a waist belt.

The Roman army's use of a buckled belt was carried through into the traditions of Anglian and other successors – cf. the splendid belt-set retrieved from the Late to Post-Roman cemetery at Mucking, Essex. Civilians, by contrast, gathered their tunics with a sash or cord, or left the garment hanging loose. The Latin (or Etruscan) word *balteus* denoted a sword belt (whether around the waist or an over-the-shoulder 'baldric'), while *cingulum* was reserved for the military waist belt. The OE *belt* derives from *balteus*, overlapping with the Germanic-derived word *gyrdel* ('girdle') for a belt with a pouch attached.

Trousers

These were in use since the Iron Age, and the early models were probably identical to the 3rd-century pair found at Thorsberg, Denmark. Iconographically, the details of legwear are often hidden beneath the tunic.

AFTERMATH OF BATTLE OF EDINGTON, AD 879
(1) King Alfred of Wessex
In the aftermath of his greatest victory, the king stands before the altar, accompanied by priests, about to present the defeated Danish *jarl* Guthrum with a gold arm-ring to signify the latter's submission. Alfred is depicted in iconography with short hair and a neatly trimmed beard. He wears a knee-length red woollen tunic with short sleeves, bordered with a vinescroll pattern embroidered in gold on red. Under this he wears a white silken undertunic with sleeves reaching the wrist, where they are edged like the overtunic. His sky-blue trousers are tight-fitting, the leather cross-gartering fastened with gilt buckles, and his soft leather shoes are buff-yellow. On his right hand he wears a gold finger ring. His dark green woollen cloak is draped over a chair behind him with the gilded disc brooch visible.
(2) West Saxon *ealdorman*
This war-seasoned senior nobleman is mainly copied from the Repton Stone, with the addition of the Coppergate helmet.

His body is protected by a waist-length, short-sleeved iron scale armour, over a knee-length under-armour garment in padded fabric worn over his green tunic. Grey trousers with a woven pattern are tucked into calf-length boots of russet leather, in Carolingian style. His sword is taken from the Abingdon specimen, and below the front of his yellowish leather belt is a long *seax* in a leather sheath, worn with the cutting edge upward. The shield resting beside him bears motifs copied from the major 9th-century Trewhiddle hoard, found down a mine near St Austell, Cornwall.
(3) Danish *jarl*
Our imagined reconstruction of Guthrum, at the moment of accepting Christianity under Alfred's sponsorship, kneels before the king, priests and altar. He is wearing a white shift which is plain apart from braid at the collar and cuffs, copied from the Maaseik embroidery. Around his waist is a loosely-tied plain sash in purple-red, and around his brow is a white silk band with the *chrism* (a Christian symbol) folded inside it.

Reconstruction of 6th-century
bridle elements from finds at
Eriswell, Suffolk. (Drawing by
Andrea Salimbeti, ex Fern)

Breeches and longer trousers were used in all the periods, as also were *braies* or hose – two fabric tubes suspended from a belt. Late manuscript images always depict the legwear as tight-fitting, often with bindings (possibly woollen or leather straps) confining them from below the knee to the ankle. Trouser colours are often off-white, but also mauve, and (as worn by Harold on the Bayeux Tapestry) dark blue.

Shoes

The 11th-century manuscripts represent kings, noblemen and royal guards with pointed shoes fitting low beneath the ankle bone (anklebone), and mainly in buff, black or brown colours.

Caps

A very early form of soft headgear is evidenced on a 5th-century ceramic figure from the Anglian cemetery at Spong Hill, Norfolk: a 'pill-box' cap similar in form to the Late Roman military *pileus pannonicus*.

A 'Phrygian' cap – raised, drawn forward, sometimes ribbed and/or 'crenellated' in profile – is often represented in 11th-century miniatures, and should not necessarily be considered as simply an artistic convention. It is mainly associated with military figures, often in battle, including royal bodyguards rather than kings themselves, and may have been made of plain leather, *cuir bouilli* or even felted wool (*Hexateuch*, folio 22r). Those of the kings' retainers are represented as high and conical, often yellow in colour or embroidered (*Hexateuch*, folio 37r).

Cloaks

The Saxons perhaps adopted specialist military capes from Roman dress, and both long cloaks and short mantles were widely worn by kings and noblemen. The cloaks of the men on the Franks Casket are typical of the garments depicted in later manuscripts: rectangular, with the upper corners fastened together by a brooch-pin at the right shoulder.

From the 9th century onwards the influence of the Carolingian court is evident in the combination of a cloak with a short tunic. The short mantle of the king and some of his retinue in 11th-century manuscript images is usually squarish or rectangular, represented in a light blue or blue-green colour, medium blue, light or olive green, medium brown, mauve, reddish-pink, even purple (*Hexateuch*, folios 38v, 47r); Harold in the Bayeux Tapestry wears an indigo cloak. Cloaks may sometimes be gold-embroidered, and this may not be an artistic convention. According to the *Vita Aedwardi* ('The Life of Edward'), in the ornamentation of the king's garments 'no count was made of the cost of precious stones, rare gems and shining pearls that were used. As regards mantles *(clamidibus)*, tunics *(tunicis)*, boots and shoes *(caligis et calciamentis)*, the amount of gold which flowed in the various complicated floral designs was not weighed…'.

Very few male brooches have been found in the earliest Anglo-Saxon male graves, so knotting two corners of the garment, or closing it with cords, may have been fashionable. However, especially in the early period, a sort of Romano-British style was diffused through Britain, and both 'crossbow' and 'quoit brooch' styles (Alfriston) were certainly used by warriors. Later brooches appear in varying types, especially for royal figures. In the Bayeux Tapestry the cloak of Harold is fastened by a penannular (incomplete ring) brooch, and brooches were usually circular from the 10th century. However, one example of variation from Winchester is rectangular with extended trefoil corners, and corresponds with the one fastening the king's cloak in the *Hexateuch*, folio 36v.

The cloak is occasionally shown fastened on the left shoulder by a circular brooch, and although this is rarer than fastening on the right (e.g. the king holding a sword in the *Hexateuch*, folio 59r), there is no reason to dismiss it. In the MS Stowe 944 the cloak of King Cnut is fastened on his left, even though he stretches out his right arm. Special decoration of the cloak and fasteners were indicators of status. The pre-battle scenes in the Bayeux Tapestry show Harold and his noblemen mainly with cloaks (scenes 1–3), distinguishing them from servants and attendants (scenes 3–6). However, as in the *Hexateuch*, there is no precise rule; an individual may be shown wearing a cloak in one scene and without it in the following miniature (scenes 7–10). Neither mantles nor cloaks are shown being worn in battle in any of the iconography.

Gilded harness mount with a garnet set in the centre, and stylized eagles' heads, found in Hampshire. Christopher Fern has studied the similar Cowbridge mount in conjunction with harness fittings from Mound 17 at Sutton Hoo, and has concluded that this piece represents a development uniting a circular mount with an originally separate *pelta*-shaped mount. This would have been used on a bridle, at the junction of the noseband and cheekpiece where three functional straps meet a decorative terminal. (PAS record HAMP-408148, licence CC BY-SA 4.0)

Hairstyles

The English love-affair with the moustache, already visible on the Repton Stone, seems to significantly pre-date its use in the Bayeux Tapestry, where it is used to distinguish the English warriors from their Norman foes. Indeed, the decoration on the face of the 7th-century Sutton Hoo helmet shows a neat moustache framing the upper lip but not extending far beyond the edges of the mouth. The 8th-century Anglo-Saxon scholar Alcuin lamented that Northumbrian men were emulating Viking style by 'trimming their hair and beard like the pagans', thus implying the

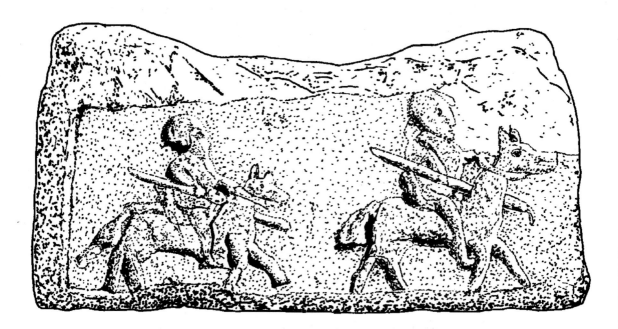

A picture stone of mounted warriors from Sockburn, Co Durham, late 9th to mid-10th century. These two Anglo–Scandinavian elite horsemen are cantering, holding in their left hands short reins to what seem to be snaffle bits, and carrying a spear in their right hands. They lack helmets, but may wear close-fitting caps. They sit on high-backed saddles, and seem to be braced back against them. The horses' long tails are knotted up. (*in situ*, Sockburn; drawing by Andrea Salimbeti, ex Hadley)

previous use of long hair and beards. Regal images in the 9th century show hair cut to collar-length and neatly trimmed beards and moustaches. In the 11th century, manuscript miniatures show Old Testament elders wearing a long 'forked' beard, either with or without moustaches.

Interestingly, some manuscript miniatures show the hair of noblemen as coloured – green, orange, or a rich deep blue (*Hexateuch*, folio 47r). In her writings on Anglo-Saxon costume Owen-Crocker says that 'the use of colour in Anglo-Saxon art is not realistic'. While it is obviously true that early iconography must always be approached with great caution, and that the pigments used on manuscripts also may well have discoloured over time, this dismissal may be too drastic. The continental Celts are reported to have sometimes dyed their hair bright red with goats' grease and beechwood ashes, or bleached it with lime water, and worn it long like a horse's mane. The plant and mineral sources of natural colourants for the skin and hair were readily available throughout England. There are contemporary reports that Saxons did dye their hair blue, as shown in the miniatures of the *Hexateuch*, though this obviously raises the question: did those writers actually see people with blue hair, or just drawings of them?

HORSEMANSHIP

Travel and combat on horseback

The Anglo-Saxon army sometimes both travelled and fought on foot (OE *feðan*, 'infantry'), but more usually travelled by horse (*eoh*). We know from various Old English poems that the saddle was part of the warrior's normal equipment. Saddle elements, spurs and bridles form one of the characteristic types of grave-goods in high-status burials – e.g. the horseman graves at Niederstotzingen (Germany) and elsewhere – but cemetery remains of horses are not found in England to the extent that they are on the continent. Warriors arrived at the field of battle on horseback, and either assembled in squadrons for the attack or dismounted and formed up on foot for defence. Presumably the men whose task it was to drive the supply wagons also had to hold the horses during fighting. Byrhtnoð, the English commander at the battle at Maldon in 991, kept his horse by him even when he had ordered the others to be removed.

Horses were widely used in warfare elsewhere in northern and western Europe from the Migration period onwards. From the subsequent Merovingian and Vendel periods there is often ample evidence for this, both in literary sources and in the iconography – e.g. the *pressblechs* from the helmets in Vendel grave 1, Sutton Hoo (Mound 17), the Staffordshire Hoard, and other examples. Among the finds of English archaeology there is some evidence from east Kent for bowmanship alongside horsemanship, from material included in high-status graves at Dover (Buckland cemetery); this may indicate that horse-archers were a recognized military force, although such graves might simply be those of huntsmen. Other graves with horses and associated with weapons were found in Suffolk (Snape, and Sutton Hoo Mound 17). Likewise, the characteristic equipment of Late Roman heavy cavalry was used in Anglo-Saxon England in the 6th and 7th centuries (although there is no evidence for heavily-armoured horsemen on the Iranian *clibanarius* model, as there is in contemporary Vendel graves).

The remarkable bronze figurine from Bradwell (Norfolk) shows a mounted warrior with shield and sword sitting on a small, sturdy horse. The figure is probably from the 7th century, and the lack of stirrups supports this early date. This fits well with an episode described in the *Historia Ecclesiastica* of Bede, when one of King Edwin's priests 'incontinently casting away vain superstition... besought the king to grant him harness and a stallion war horse *(equus emissarius)* whereon he might mount and come to destroy the [pagan] idols. For it was not before lawful for a priest of the sacrifices either to wear harness or to ride on other than a mare. Girded therefore with a sword *(gladius)* about his loins, he took a spear *(lancea)* in his hand, and, mounting the king's war horse, set forth against the idols'.

Mounted military forces formed the backbone of Carolingian armies from the 8th century onwards, being indispensable for leaders with a large territory to administer and defend. This fact was known to Anglo-Saxon travellers – pilgrims and nobles making the long land passage to Rome – although the

Anglo-Saxon stirrup, 11th century, from southern England. Decorated with a distinctive technique of iron inlay, it is of a type perhaps introduced during the renewed Viking attacks at the end of the 10th century, and visible on the Bayeux Tapestry. (Metropolitan Museum, New York, inv. no. 47.100.23; Museum photo, public domain)

military hazards faced by the English at that time were rather small-scale when compared to the frontiers of the Carolingian regime.

To be of service, horses had to be trained not to flee from the commotion of battle; they had to be quite large – taller than a man's shoulder if the rider was to have a real advantage of height; and they had to have enough stamina to keep going after the opposition began to flag. The typical Anglo-Saxon horse as evidenced in the burial records was around 13–15 hands tall (about 1.4m/4 ft 7ins) at the shoulder, and weighed around 300–500kg/600–1,100 lbs, making it a hefty animal with considerable presence.

Spurs are widely attested from the 6th century onward. Archaeological evidence for the use of stirrups begins in the Middle Saxon period and it is definitely attested in 11th-century miniatures, confirmed by some artefacts. The saddle is sometimes represented only as a fur or fleece cover, and harness in the manuscript illustrations is usually dark brown. The *Hexateuch* shows the king and his retainers on horseback (folios 25), using both stirrups and spurs. The saddles seem to be of fringed fur; harness is brown leather with pendant strips, and small *phalerae* at the ear intersection of the bridle.

Some literary evidence has been cited to suggest that the Anglo-Saxons were not used to fighting on horseback, but the many counter-arguments have been presented in scholarly debate for more than a century. The three textual sources for this notion are the poem *The Battle of Maldon* probably written shortly after 991; John of Worcester's account of the battle of Hereford (1055); and the events of 1066 as recorded in the *ASC*, in the writings of Snorri Sturluson, and in the Bayeux Tapestry. All these sources are relatively late, and therefore may not be typical of earlier times. One scholar believes that the Maldon and Hastings texts have been a 'major hindrance to the study of how battles were fought … [they] have not simply had a substantial impact on our interpretation of warfare, they have *defined* Anglo-Saxon warfare. Both Maldon and Hastings were defensive battles in which a firm stand had to be taken against an invading foe. In neither case did the English commander choose to leave his men mounted – and it is no coincidence that both were heavy defeats'. (Cathers, 2002)

The evidence of the Bayeux Tapestry is often used to generalize from the particular: that since the English army at Hastings was not mounted, it could *only* fight on foot, while the Normans preferred fighting from horseback. Yet during several episodes depicted on the Tapestry Harold is shown on horseback, including accompanying Duke William in the battle of Dinan, and there is no suggestion that he was an inferior horseman. While it is unwise to infer from this that the English were all equally comfortable on horseback, it

G AFTERMATH OF BATTLE OF BRUNANBURH, AD 937
(1) King Athelstan of England
The king is about to distribute the spoils of victory among his warriors in a meadhall. According to his portrait in MS.183 fol.1v (Cambridge), Athelstan had a slender build and fair hair and beard. He wears an *alba*-white tunic with bands of gold thread brocade at the hem, cuffs and flanking the vent on the chest. Over this he wears a short blue silken mantle clasped at his right shoulder with a gold disc brooch. His sword, copied from the Chertsey Museum specimen (CHYMS 2645), is carried by his attendant *ealdorman* (2).
(2) Mercian *ealdorman*
This warrior's equipment is copied largely from the Norbury

Stone sculpture. The helmet is based on the Yarm specimen, but crested as on the Norbury Stone. His olive-green tunic, hemmed with a band of bright multicoloured embroidery in Carolingian style, is almost obscured by his padded fabric or leather armour with decorative stitched volutes. The multicoloured leggings or hose are clearly of woven fabric, probably wool.
(3) *Scop*
Seated on a low stool, the middle-aged poet is preparing to declaim a poem of praise for the king and his loyal warriors. The harp is of waxed wood, with decorative interlaced panels and roundels carved lightly into the surface. For travel it would be carried in a waterproof leather bag with a shoulder-strap.

does suggest that among both the Norman and the English elite proficiency at riding was one of the expected accomplishments. Without the example of the images presented in the Tapestry, it is unlikely that historians would have placed such emphasis on Norman cavalry; the *Carmen de Hastingae Proelio/Carmen Windonis* (believed to date from 1067) does not stress any such tactical gulf between the two armies.

A rigid distinction between 'cavalry' and 'infantry' is characteristic of both more ancient and later medieval military tactics, and may have had no real bearing on the equipment and deployment of early medieval warriors. It has long been known that Anglo-Saxon forces were able to acquire horses in large numbers when necessary – for example, when countering the Danes – but they did not harbour an image of 'cavalry' as implicitly superior to footsoldiers. The same men who fought toe-to-toe with the Danes in the shieldwall later pursued them on horseback when they fled (see below, 'Brunanburh, 937'). Monuments such as the 8th-century Aberlemno Stone clearly show mounted warriors wearing Anglian helmets engaging in fighting, and there is no reason to believe that the images represent anything other than the contemporary understanding of a battle.

Standards and flags
Military standards or pennants were used throughout the Anglo-Saxon period.

Famous in Bede's history (HE, XVI) is the mention of the *tufa* of King Edwin: 'And moreover, he had such excellency of glory in the kingdom that not only in battle were banners *(Vexilla)* borne before him, but in time of peace too a standard-bearer *(signifer)* was accustomed to go before him whensoever he rode about the cities, townships or shires with his thanes; yea, even when he passed through the streets to any place there was wont to be carried before him that kind of banner which the Romans call *Tufa* but the English *Thuuf*. This text shows that the Anglians carried *vexilla* (probably

A copper-alloy mount representing a warrior wearing a horned helmet, early 7th century. The wide diffusion of images with horned helmets in England and Scandinavia in the 6th and 7th centuries may support the idea that they were not necessarily an artistic convention, but an actual form perhaps used during pagan rituals. Here, the horns meet at the apex in conjoined bird's-head terminals to form a ring, and the face has a large drooping mouth and perhaps a moustache and a pointed beard. The figure is wearing a garment with a cross-over front opening, and has the arms bent at the elbow to grip two spears at shoulder height. Motifs of figures with horns and carrying a pair of spears are well known from early 7th-century art; parallels include the Finglesham buckle. (PAS record FAHG-8EAAA3, licence CC BY-SA 4.0; drawing by Lindsay Kerr)

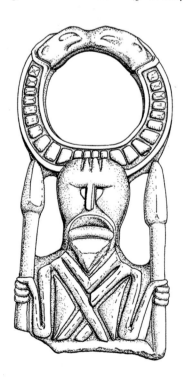

in the shape of Roman squared, fringed flags hanging from a crossbar, as still visible in Carolingian miniatures); but also that as a personal standard the king had a *tufa*, i.e. a spearshaft from which hung a tuft of feathers, *ex confertis plumarum globis* (Ducange, *Latin Dictionary*, p.204) or horsehair.

From an early scene in *Beowulf*, we hear that the troop of men accompanying Beowulf to Denmark had given up hope of victory:... *ac him dryhtenforgeaf, wigsped agewiofu...* (*Beowulf*, l. 696–7); 'but the lord gave to them, webs of war-might'. The nature of the poetically described *wigsped agewiofu* ('weavings of war-speed') is probably some form of banner with magical powers. A belief in the totemic nature of the battle-flag is implied in the later saga of Olaf Tryggvason, who received a standard from a supernatural female with the words 'Now accept a banner, for I have made [it] with all my magical skill, and I foresee that he before whom it is borne must be victorious, but he must die who bears it.' The saga continues: 'The banner was made with much fine work and resplendent craftsmanship. It was made in the form of a raven, and whenever the wind blew the banner, it was as if the raven stretched its wings for flight'.

The military standards shown on 10th-century English coins and the Bayeux Tapestry are mainly small, rectangular, and with a dagged trailing edge, echoing 'barbarian' standards shown on Roman coins centuries earlier. The simple, geometric blazons depicted (mainly crosses and circles) could easily have been made either by appliqué shapes or by embroidery. However, the Tapestry's depiction of what appears to be Harold's personal standard is in the form of a reddish dragon (the dragon of Wessex?), which is probably of the Late Roman *draco* type based on the 'windsock' principle – a moulded beast-head with gaping mouth, to which a tubular fabric 'tail' was attached in order to inflate when in motion.

The other mentioned standard of Harold at the battle of Hastings was the so-called *Ravageur du Monde*, which presents a puzzle. According to Guillaume de Poitiers (II, 31), it represented an armoured man embroidered in gold (*hominis armati imaginem intextam habens ex auro purissimo*). No other reference to it is known, and its real appearance is still a mystery, but Guillaume wrote that Duke William sent it to Pope Alexander II (might it even still be hidden among the Vatican treasure?).

Picture stone of a helmeted warrior from Sockburn, County Durham; Anglo–Scandinavian, AD 950–975. His head has been tooled away, but he seems to have worn a sharply pointed helmet, as paralleled in carvings at Staveley and Middleton. With one hand he holds a spear upright, and at his waist is a sword apparently with curving guard quillons, but the hilt is broken. (*in situ*, Sockburn; drawing by Andrea Salimbeti, ex Hadley)

FOUR MAJOR BATTLES

Catraeth, *c.*600

This battle is the subject of a long poem in Old Welsh *(Y Gododdin),* which details the main events in heroic terms. It took place in around 600 in the area of modern Catterick, Yorkshire. The attackers comprised a cavalry troop of 'three hundred' warriors raised by the Gododdin, a North British tribe whose name represents the Iron-Age people known as *Votadini*. The Gododdin force comprised warriors drawn from all over the area called *Hen*

Ogledd ('The Old North') – northern Romano–British kingdoms, possibly including Gwynedd in North Wales. It is generally thought that a force of 300 horsemen would be too small for a major military campaign, and that the number had been chosen for poetic reasons to demonstrate the heroism of the outnumbered Britons in mounting an attack against overwhelming odds. Alternatively, the horsemen may have been only the elite warriors whom the poet thought worthy of mention, while disregarding their accompanying infantry.[1]

The British leader – perhaps Mynyddog Mwynfawr – gathered a large force of chosen champions from across the Brythonic kingdoms. He feasted them at Din Eidyn (Edinburgh) for a year, prepared them for battle, and then launched an attack on Catraeth. The defenders were seemingly Angles who had recently advanced into Deira and captured that stronghold. *Y Gododdin* mentions fighting both on horseback and on foot; the battle resulted in a resounding victory for the Angles, from which the northern Romano–British never recovered.

The tale does not figure in any surviving Anglo-Saxon sources, but the written records of Northumbria are no longer plentiful; what we know of its early history is dependent on the writings of Bede, a monk of Jarrow, whose text *Historia Ecclesiastica Gentis Anglorum* recounts the establishment of the Christian church in Northumbria. A critical Anglian military victory such as the poem relates would certainly have been celebrated by Anglo-Saxons in song for generations afterwards, but may not have been considered relevant to or desirable in Bede's history of the church.

Edington, 878

A Danish army led by a *jarl* named Guthrum attempted to invade Wessex from its base in East Anglia. The Danes had already occupied several important towns and evaded the attempts of King Alfred to bring them to battle, always preferring to move beyond the reach of his forces. The Danes had taken payments to leave the country and had sworn solemn oaths that they would make peace with Wessex, but never actually did more than move on to their next target in Britain or on the continent.

Alfred's own household was caught by a surprise attack over midwinter when they were celebrating Christmas at Chippenham (Wiltshire), in what was the holiest time of year for the Christians, and the season when pagans relaxed with their families after the end of the agricultural year. Alfred, his family and a small retinue escaped the attack, but had to seek refuge in the Somerset marshes at a hunting lodge on the island of Athelney, probably a minor royal hall. Rather than surrender, choose a life in exile, or buy the enemy off yet again, Alfred summoned his followers to meet him at Egbert's Stone (*Ecgbryhtesstan*, location unknown), and from there he led them to Edington (*Eþandun*), where battle took place. Against expectation, the West Saxons overcame the Danes and drove them from the field. The Vikings retreated to a nearby fortified town, where the king besieged them and forced their surrender after two weeks.

Alfred insisted that the Danish leader become a Christian as a condition of his capitulation, with the king as his sponsor – which

Another 10th-century picture stone from Sockburn, depicting an elite warrior wearing a helmet and carrying a shield and long spear. The crested helmet can hardly be associated with the Vikings; its shape more closely recalls the Anglo-Saxon tradition of the Wollaston and Coppergate helmets, fitted with wide cheek-guards. (*in situ* Sockburn; photo Raffaele D'Amato)

1 For a more detailed analysis, see Elite 248, *Post-Roman Kingdoms: 'Dark Ages' Gaul & Britain, AD 450–800.*

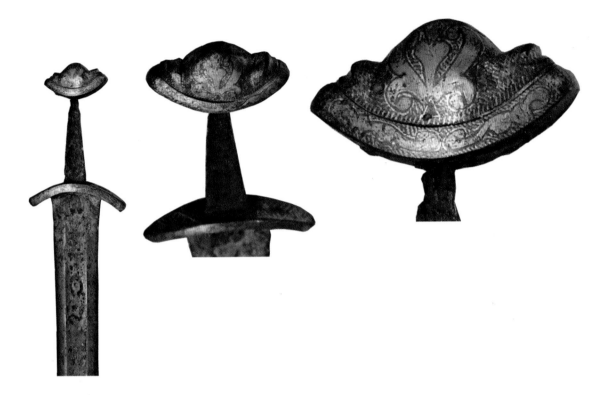

automatically made Alfred Guthrum's political and spiritual overlord. A negotiated peace followed in which Wessex consolidated its power, and eventually drove the Danes from the south of England.

Details of a beautiful 10th-century Anglo-Saxon sword found in the Thames in 1840. It shows a fine inlay design on the fullered pommel, and the blade carries a runic inscription. (Tullie House Museum and Art Gallery Trust; photo courtesy of Matt Bunker)

Brunanburh, 937

An alliance of Scandinavian *jarls* and Irish (Hiberno–Norse) princes joined forces with the leading men of the kingdom of York, and attempted to prevent King Athelstan from consolidating all English territory under his sole rule. Resentment at the growing power of Winchester and its satellites (the commercial port of London and the spiritual centre of Canterbury) encouraged the northern chieftains and the Archbishop of York to attempt to create a break-away state based on the wealth generated by commercial trade routes stretching east across the North Sea to Norway and Denmark, and west across the Irish Sea to Dublin.

Olaf Guthrithson, the king of the Dublin Vikings, made an alliance with Constantine II, king of the Scots, and King Owain of Strathclyde, to combine forces: their aim was to bring Athelstan down, but it is not clear whether one or other of them planned to assume supreme command of the alliance in the event of their victory.

The English were at this time still more often loyal to their older political groupings (Wessex, Mercia, Northumbria, Kent, and the rest) than to the king and the wider English nation. Athelstan was a member of the Wessex royal line – grandson of Alfred the Great – but he grew up in the Midlands, and was thus Mercian by birth. His father, Edward the Elder, had undertaken the reconquest of territory from the Danes, but in so doing he had sometimes had to impose an unwelcome southern authority on areas outside the heartland of Wessex. His task as king was to unite all the various local identities behind a common Englishness, overriding the centrifugal tendencies of provincial leaders and magnates. The threat to all English territory posed by the power of the enemy alliance now offered him an opportunity to overcome this hesitant suspicion.

Athelstan's army moved north to meet the gathering forces of the Scots and Hiberno-Norse, and the ensuing battle resulted in the capture or slaughter of almost the entire invading army. The Old English poem now called *Brunanburh* records the outline of events in heroic terms. It opens with the resounding statement 'Here Athelstan the king, lord of heroes and ring-giver of champions, and his brother likewise, Eadmund the atheling, won lifelong glory in combat with their swords' edges around Brunanburh. They smashed the shieldwall, hewed war-shields with the leavings of hammers [swords] ... The attackers fell, both the men of the Scots and the seaborne forces ...'.

The poem specifically mentions the great deeds of the West Saxons ('for the whole day the West Saxons in mounted troops were on the track of the hated people') and the Mercians ('the Mercians did not refuse hard hand-to-hand fighting to any of those champions who sought our land with Olaf who had come over the churning waters in the hold of a ship'). The combined Wessex–Mercian army achieved a convincing victory which swept away most of the leaders of the invaders, either dead or powerless and obliged to flee ('five young kings lay slain by swords on the battlefield, likewise seven of Olaf's earls and countless warriors of the seamen and Scots). There the Northmen's prince was put to flight, compelled by necessity back to his ship's keel with a small bodyguard ... Likewise also the experienced leader Constantine came back from the rout to his kinsmen in the north, the grey-haired warmaker'... '[He] had no cause to boast of that clash of swords, that old invader, any more than did Olaf ...'. The mention of mounted West Saxons is interesting, since it clearly implies that they were deployed as cavalry to break up, harry and pursue the Vikings and Scots.

H HAROLD GODWINESON, AD 1065–66

(1) King Harold II

Harold is about 45 years old, but very fit and active; he has short-cut fair hair and a moustache. Here we imagine him arguing with his younger brother Tostig, whom he would banish in October 1065. Harold wears a ringmail *byrnie* which reaches to his knees, and is split front and back for ease of riding; the Bayeux Tapestry shows the edges of the thrown-back hood *(coif)*, elbow-length sleeves and lower hem trimmed with leather. On the forearms note his linen tunic woven in horizontal stripes of white and deep blue. His helmet is conical, of the Norman type with a broad nasal, and the Tapestry shows it partly lacquered red. His sword is at his left hip, and the Tapestry shows the scabbard as passing through a slit in his *byrnie*.

(2) Royal *húskarl*

The description by William of Malmesbury (of housecarls offered to Hardacnut by Godwin in 1041) gives us a vivid image of these royal guardsmen: 'It was a ship beaked with gold, having 80 soldiers on board, who had two bracelets on either arm, each weighing 16 ounces of gold; on their heads were gilt helmets; on their left shoulder they carried a Danish axe, with an iron spear in their right hand; and... they were equipped with such arms... that splendour vying with terror might conceal the steel beneath the gold'. This member of

Harold's bodyguard sports gold arm-rings on each wrist. Over a fabric or leather hood he wears a conical helmet ornamented with silvering or tinning and gilding. He has a leather coat covered with iron discs applied in rows rather than interlinked ringmail. On his left shoulder he rests a large 'Danish' battleaxe; the varied iconography sometimes shows a very long haft, and these weapons were reportedly used effectively against mounted opponents' horses. In his right hand he holds a 'hunting' spear; both weapons are copied from English 11th-century archaeological finds. Note the spurs, confirming that he rode to the battlefield.

(3) Tostig Godwineson, Earl of Northumbria

Tostig was one of Harold's younger brothers, whose appointment as Earl of Northumbria proved unpopular with the northern elite. When they rebelled against him in 1065 Harold soon deposed and outlawed him, but he raided and plotted ceaselessly to secure his return. Eventually he persuaded King Harald Hardrada of Norway to lead a landing on the English north-east coast, but both were killed by Harold's army at Stamford Bridge on 25 September 1066, just 19 days before the battle of Hastings. His tunic and semicircular mantle are conventional for an 11th-century *æpeling*. In his right hand he holds the *draco* standard, copied (like most of the figure) from the Bayeux Tapestry.

The Battersea sword, late 10th or early 11th century, decorated with copper-alloy inlay; this ornamentation resembles that on several high-quality stirrup-iron finds. An early 11th-century date is suggested by the acanthus ornament of the pommel, which is quite close to designs in the Winchester School of painting. (Pitt-Rivers Museum, Oxford: inv. no. P.R. 1555-2580: PLo II, A, B; photo courtesy of Matt Bunker)

Athelstan's power was not open to challenge after this victory, and he began using the words *Rex Totius Britanniae* ('King of All Britain') on his coinage. The resounding success of combined English forces under a king with a foot in both Wessex and Mercian camps was significant in creating or consolidating the new English state.

The site of the battle is disputed, with many possibilities put forward between the Wirral and the south Midlands. Many scholars believe that the site must be on or close to the Great North Road (the modern A1), and probably north of the river Humber. This would place it in the great 'war zone' of 10th-century Britain, between the area dominated by York and the Anglo-Saxon kingdom already formed from the political union of Wessex and Mercia, which extended from the Channel coast into the Midlands as far as the Humber.

A later Icelandic account of a battle called Vinheiðr in *Egilssaga Skallagrimsonar* appears to relate to the same conflict. It gives many interesting details of the disposition of troops and the events of the day, in which the saga's hero Egil played a prominent part as a mercenary on the Anglo-Saxon side, and was supposedly richly rewarded by King Athelstan. The Anglo-Saxon celebration of the victory in the *Anglo-Saxon Chronicle* compares its significance to the original triumphs which had allowed the Anglo-Saxons to establish themselves in Britain.

Maldon, 991

After decades of consolidation of Anglo-Saxon power in England under the Wessex dynasty, and its development as a powerful economic and military force, new waves of social disruption in Scandinavia resulted in a second phase of aggressive Viking activity. Coastal raiding gave way to the manoeuvres of a large seaborne army which ravaged the English east coast. An attack on the mercantile centre at Ipswich (Suffolk) was followed by the Vikings taking up a safe position on an island in the river Blackwater, Essex.

The local *ealdorman*, Byrhtnoth, gathered his forces to try to dislodge them; he was at this time over 60 years old, but still very active in national affairs. Among the Vikings may have been Olafr Tryggvason, then a young Norwegian warlord. After exchanges of archery the Vikings were allowed to cross from the island to the mainland in order to ensure that they would fight rather than sail away, and this overconfident tactical mistake resulted in a grave defeat for the locals. Byrhtnoth was cut down in the fighting, but his men fought on around his body and refused to surrender.

These events were recorded in a long epic poem of which just a few verses survive. After Byrhtnoth's death the king, Æthelred II (known to history as

'the Unready', meaning 'the Ill-Advised'), offered the invaders money to buy peace, and for several years levied a burdensome tax to pay for this – the *Denegeld* (Danegeld). Needless to say, this was not the end of England's Viking troubles (see Select Chronology).

The 'Penrith Crucifixion' plaque, 10th century. This extraordinary monument shows three warriors around the cross of Our Lord, all wearing conical helmets (at least two with a nasal) and carrying spears. This is one of the earliest English artworks showing the style of helmet usually visible in 11th century iconography. The spear-bearer (bottom right), seems to wear quilted armour. (Kendal Museum, Cumbria, inv. no. 0030/94T; photo (c) Corpus of Anglo-Saxon Stone Sculpture, photographer T. Middlemass)

SELECT BIBLIOGRAPHY

For reasons of space, we can list here only the main primary sources (including commentaries), and a limited selection of relevant secondary sources. A much fuller Bibliography of academic publications can be found on the Osprey Publishing website, by following: www.ospreypublishing.com/eli_253_bibliography.

Abbreviated references used in text

AJ   *Antiquaries' Journal*
Arch. Cant.   *Archaeologia Cantiana*
ASC   Savage, A., *The Anglo-Saxon Chronicles (etc.)*
ASE   *Anglo-Saxon England*
ASSAH   *Anglo-Saxon Studies in Archaeology & History*
AWLSK   *(Mededelingen van de Koninklijke) Academie voor Wettenschapen, Letteren en Schone Kunsten (van Belgie)*
EJA   *European Journal of Archaeology*
HE   Bede, *Ecclesiastical History*, ed & trans Colgrave & Mynors
JEGP   *Journal of English and Germanic Philology*
JIES   *Journal of Indo-European Studies*
Med. Arch.   *Medieval Archaeology*
NOWELE   *North West European Language Evolution*
PMLA   *Publications of the Modern Language Association*
RGA   *Reallexicon der Germanischen Altertumskunde*
TPAPA   *Transaction & Proceedings of the American Philological Association*

MAIN SOURCES

Almond, T.L., 'The Whitby Life of St Gregory' in *Downside Review* 23, NS 4 (1904) pp. 15–29

Bede (ed King, J. E.), *Opera Historica/ Ecclesiastic History of the English Nation* (Cambridge, 1962)

Bede (ed & trans Colgrave, B., & Mynors, R.A.B.), *Ecclesiastical History of the English People* (Oxford, 1969)

British History and the Welsh annals, ed Morris, J., History from the Sources, 8 (London & Chichester, 1980)

Canu Taliesin, ed Williams, I. (Cardiff, 1960)

'Chronicle of the Princes' in *Archaeologica Cambrensis*, Vol X, 3rd series (London, 1864) pp.1–143

Clancy, J.P., *Earliest Welsh Poetry* (London & New York, 1970)

Clhwch and Olwen: An Edition and Study of the Oldest Arthurian Text, ed Bromwich, R. & Simon Evans, D. (Cardiff, 1992)

Cunedda, Cynan, Cadwallon, Cynddylan: Four Welsh Poems and Britain 383–655, ed Koch, J.T. (Aberystwyth, 2013)

Eddius Stephanus (ed Colgrave, B.), *The Life of Bishop Wilfred* (Cambridge, 1927)

The Four Ancient Books of Wales, Vols I–II, ed Skene, W.F. (Edinburgh, 1868)

Geoffrey of Monmouth, *Historia Regum Britanniae, a Variant Version Edited from Manuscripts,* ed Hammer, J. (Medieval Academy of America, 57; Cambridge, 1951)

Geoffrey of Monmouth (ed & trans Thorpe, L.), *The History of the Kings of Britain* (Harmondsworth, 1968)

Geoffrey of Monmouth (ed & trans Thompson, A.), *The History of the Kings of Britain* (Cambridge, Ontario, 1999)

The Historia Regum Britanniae of Geoffrey of Monmouth, III: a Summary Catalogue of the Manuscripts, ed Crick, J.C. (Cambridge; Brewer, 1989)

(Gildas) *Opus novum. Gildas Britannus monarchus, cui sapientis cognomentum est inditum, 'De calamitate, excidio et conquestu Britanniae', quam Angliam nunc vocant, author uetustus a multis desyderatus et nuper in gratiam d. Cuthberti Tonstalli Lond. episcopi formulis excusus* (London, 1525)

Gildas, *The Ruin of Britain etc.* (London, 1899)

Gildas (ed Winterbottom, M.), *The Ruin of Britain and Other Works* (London & Chichester, 1978)

Giles, J.A., *The Works of Gildas and Nennius, translated from Latin, and with the former translations carefully compared and corrected* (London, 1841)

Gough-Cooper, H.W. (ed), *Annales Cambriae*, the A text, from British Library, Harley MS 3859, ff. 190r–193r (Welsh Chronicle Research Group, 2015)

Gough-Cooper, H.W. (ed), *Annales Cambriae*, the B text, from London, National Archives, MS E164/1, pp. 2–26 (Welsh Chronicle Research Group, 2015)

Gough-Cooper, H.W. (ed), *Annales Cambriae*, the C text, from London, British Library, Cotton MS, Domitian A, I., ff. 138r–155r (Welsh Chronicle Research Group, 2015)

Gough-Cooper, H.W. (ed), *Annales Cambriae*, the D text, from Exeter Cathedral MS 3514, pp. 523–528 (Welsh Chronicle Research Group, 2015)

Gregory of Tours (trans & intro Thorpe, L.), *Historia Francorum* (London, 1974)

Y Gododin (ed & trans Williams, J.A.): *a poem on the battle of Cattraeth by Aneurin, a Welsh Bard of the Sixth Century, with an English translation and numerous historical and critical annotations* (London, 1852)

The Gododdin of Aneirin (ed Koch, J.): *Text and Context from Dark Age North Britain* (Cardiff; University of Wales Press, 1997)

http://www.bl.uk/manuscripts/Viewer.aspx?ref=cotton_ms_claudius_b_iv_fs001r

Nennius (trans Giles, J.A.), *History of the Britons/Historia Brittonum* (Ontario, 2000)

Notitia Dignitatum (ed Seeck, O.), *accedunt Notitia Urbis Constantinopolitanae et laterculi Provinciarum* (Berlin, 1876)

Orosius (trans Fear, A.T.), *Seven Books of History Against the Pagans* (Liverpool University Press, 2010)

Paolo Diacono/Paul the Deacon (ed Crivellucci, A.), *Historia Romana* (Rome, 1914)

Rowland, J., *Early Welsh Saga Poetry* (Cambridge, 1990)

Savage, A., *The Anglo-Saxon Chronicles: The authentic voices of England, from the time of Julius Caesar to the coronation of Henri II* (London, 2000)

'David and Goliath', in a detail from an 11th-century manuscript. Again, Goliath is represented with the typical nasal-guard conical helmet of the period, and ringmail armour. (British Library, Harley Psalter MS 603; photo Raffaele D'Amato, courtesy of the Library)

'St George killing the Dragon', an illuminated capital from the 11th-century Grimbald Gospel. Note the dotted decoration of the tunic. (British Library, Ms. Add. 34890, folio 158r ; photo Raffaele D'Amato, courtesy of the Library)

Sidonius Appollinaris, in Migne, J.P., *Patrologiae Cursus Completus*, Latin series, Vol XVIII (1844)

Sidonius, *Poems and Letters* (ed Anderson, W.B.), 2 vols (Harvard University Press, 1963)

Thorpe, B., *The Anglo-Saxon Chronicle/Rerum Britannicarum Medii Ævi Scriptores*, 2 vols (London, 1861)

Trioedd Yny Prydein/The Welsh Triads, ed & trans Bromwich, R. (Cardiff, 1978)

William of Malmesbury's chronicle of the Kings of England, from the earliest period to the reign of King Stephen (London, 1847)

SECONDARY SOURCES

Abels, R., *Lordship and Military Obligation in Anglo-Saxon England* (London, 1988)

Ager, B., 'The Smaller Variants of the Anglo-Saxon Quoit Brooch', in *ASSAH*, Vol 4 (Oxford, 1985) pp.1–35

Allen-Brown, R., *The Battle of Hastings* (1980; r/p Morillo, 1999 – qv)

Arnold, C.J., *An Archaeology of the Early Anglo-Saxon Kingdoms* (London, 1997)

Ausenda, G. (ed), *After Empire: Towards an Ethnology of Europe's Barbarians* (Woodbridge, 1995)

Bachrach, B.S., *Armies and Politics in the Early Medieval West* (Aldershot, 1993)

Baker, P.S., *The Beowulf Reader* (New York, 2000)

Batholow, P., 'Continental connections: Angles, Saxons and Jutes in Bede and Procopius', in *ASSAH*, Vol 13 (Oxford, 2006)

Bazelmans, J., *By Weapons made Worthy: Lords, Retainers and their Relationship in Beowulf* (Amsterdam, 1999)

Blackmore, L., *The Prittlewell Prince: the Discovery of a Rich Anglo-Saxon Burial in Essex* (London, 2004)

Bruce-Mitford, R., *The Sutton Hoo Ship-Burial*, 3 vols (London, 1975, 1978 & 1983)

Cathers, C., *An Examination of the Horse in Anglo-Saxon England* (PhD dissertation; Reading, 2002)

Chadwick Hawkes, S. (ed), *Weapons and Warfare in Anglo-Saxon England* (Oxford University Committee for Archaeology, Monograph No. 21; Oxford, 1989)

Chaney, W.A., *The Cult of Kingship in Anglo-Saxon England: The Transition from Paganism to Christianity* (Manchester, 1970)

Cross, P.J., 'Horse Burial in First Millenium AD Britain: Issues of Interpretation', in *EJA*, Vol 14 (2011) pp.180–209

Evans, S., *Lords of Battle: Image and Reality of the Comitatus in Dark-Age Britain* (Woodbridge, 1997)

Fern, C., Dickinson, T. & Webster, L. (eds), *The Staffordshire Hoard: An Anglo-Saxon Treasure. Research Report of the Society of Antiquaries of London*, Vol 80 (London, 2019)

Gilmour, B., 'Swords, Seaxes and Saxons: Pattern-Welding and Edged Weapon Technology from Late Roman Britain to Anglo-Saxon England', in Henig & Smith eds (2007) pp. 91–109

Halsall, G., *Warfare and Society in the Barbarian West, 400–900* (London, 2003)

Harvey Wood, H., *The Battle of Hastings: The Fall of Anglo-Saxon England* (London, 2008)

Higham, N.J., *The English Conquest: Gildas and Britain in the Fifth Century* (Manchester, 1994)

Hines, J., *The Scandinavian Character of Anglian England in the Pre-Viking Period* (BAR Publishing, British series; Oxford, 1984)

Horovitz, D., *Notes and Materials on the Battle of Tettenhall 910 AD and Other Researches* (Stafford, 2010)

Morillo, S., *The Battle of Hastings: Sources and Interpretations* (Woodbridge, 1999)

Mortimer, P., *Woden's Warriors* (Ely, 2011)

Pollington, S., *Anglo-Saxon Burial Mounds* (Swaffham, 2008)

Scragg, D. (ed), *The Battle of Maldon* (Manchester, 1981)

Underwood, R., *Anglo-Saxon Weapons and Warfare* (Stroud, 2000)

Webster, L. & Backhouse, J., *The Making of England: Anglo-Saxon Art and Culture AD 600–900* (London, 1991)

INDEX

Note: page numbers in **bold** refer to illustrations, captions and plates.